THE SMARTERCHARTER CATAMARAN GUIDE: CARIBBEAN

Insiders' Tips for Confident Bareboat Cruising

MICHAEL DOMICAN AND DAVID BLACKLOCK

Illustrated by
KIM DOWNING

NOTE: We refer frequently to "the Skipper" and define the action aboard ship as being under their direction. All true—but the information is accessible and applicable to any sailor, regardless of experience. On a bareboat charter, the person whose name is on the contract and who is responsible for the well-being and safety of the vessel and occupants undertakes that they, or members of their party, are suitably qualified to operate the vessel. The position of "Skipper" is a role that any suitably experienced person might fill with the consent and presumed supervision of the nominal charterer—for training, practice, or crew development purposes.

Information and preparation are the keys to happy sailing in any situation.

Welcome Aboard

Background

R um, pirates, rebellion, and hell-raising. These few words are all it takes to summon up the history of a region steeped in scandal and mystery—the Hollywood version, anyway.

With a picturesque narrative of piratical intrigue and swashbuckling adventure (and that's without mention of the dark side of the Trans-Atlantic trade) the Caribbean has long been one of the world's most desirable sailing destinations. The physical characteristics that historically made the region so amenable to sailing ships—consistent wind from the right quarter at a reliable strength, fresh water, plentiful sea life—still hold true today. Freebooters, Privateers, Buccaneers—these marine gangsters loaded and unloaded their cargoes of bountiful booty while chasing one another from island to island for 200-plus years.

Recreational sailors have been following the same routes and enjoying the same ideal conditions for more than 50 years, savoring the pleasures but without some of the fearsome hazards.

Amenities such as quality repair and maintenance facilities, clean fuel, good hotels and restaurants, excellent air transport—all of which are available in many (though not all) of the islands—have brought (or followed) the charter business to the region. In addition, the peak time for charter visits—the Winter/Spring period—is often snow-bound and usually chilly in the northern regions of Europe and the Americas.

LATELY, though, such considerations have been overshadowed by the tragic events of 2017 and after, when hurricanes destroyed the infrastructure on many of the islands and demolished or damaged hundreds—thousands—of boats and along with them much of the charter industry.

That the industry, along with the islands, has survived numerous challenges in recent years is to a great extent a testament to the resilience and determination of the Caribbean people. They have had a long acquaintance with adversity—most residents can tell a tale of re-building, of picking up the pieces.

Those who know and love the region have come back to show their support and to honor the determination of the residents. And some who have yet to make their first trip to the islands will see a good reason to come. Many of the smaller charter businesses are family concerns and they have deep roots in their places of residence.

Today, marinas and hotels are in the process of rebuilding. New ventures are being planned and old favorites are being re-imagined and re-built. It's not simply that things will be restored to the way they were, they are being revamped to accommodate the new realities. Charter companies are restocking their fleets—virtually all the major firms have brand-new boats in the water—and adding new options to fit the changing mood of their customers. While everyone keeps a wary eye on the weather map.

THE DISASTERS of 2017 and later, combined with a changing demographic, gave charter operators an opportunity to configure their fleets more in line with a developing market. The dominance of the sailing catamaran is near complete, as the emphasis on comfort and amenities has overshadowed the former, more salty, requirements of the dedicated sailing crew.

Where the customer had previously most often been an experienced sailor, the new reality encompasses the fact that while there are a considerable number of skilled boat operators, there are fewer experienced crew.

And time is a luxury. It's all very well to potter along at 4 or 5 knots, but to do so at a high angle of heel—and not always in the desired direction—is too big an ask. A leisurely holiday has to be balanced against the pressures of ever-increasing workloads and the temptations of a dozen other possibilities. And many people 'on vacation' find themselves checking into work at some point every day or two.

The charter companies found creative ways to accommodate this new reality. The expansion of sailing fleets to encompass catamarans has allowed for a greater number of guests in roomy hotel-type accommodation. The boats sailed flat, they were fast, and there was plenty of space to relax. Some guests didn't even bother to sail all that much! Or when they did, it was off the wind at a fast clip and at an angle that doesn't require constant crew effort.

AND WITH A GENERATOR pumping out the amps--though not while underway, of course—everyone had Wi-Fi, the air conditioning was blasting, everything worked. While pressure on the infrastructure—crowded anchorages, larger yachts, more demand for services and amenities—may be reduced in the short term, a new balance is being struck. Vacationing families—and increasingly the flotilla groups—are finding ways to solve the riddle of maximizing their pleasure while enjoying the wonders of the region and having memorable aquatic experiences.

For many, the answer has been the fastest growing category of sailing yacht, the Catamaran.

Getting Started

C hartering a yacht in a new location is a bit like renting an unfamiliar car in a foreign country. You know how to drive and you know how to read a map—in fact you have a trusty electronic assistant to help with that part. But it's the size of the vehicle, the other traffic, the unfamiliar signs, the roundabouts, and the overpasses that give you pause.

Do I turn left or right here? Is that a good place to park? What does that sign mean? The *gas-oil*, is that diesel or petrol? Oops, I mean gas—or do I? As with driving abroad, it's the first day or two that are the most challenging—plus coping with driving on the opposite side of the road, or with a confusing signage system. But by the end of a week, you're charging down the Autobahn like you were born to it.

You can read all the books, study up on the regions, talk to friends who have done it before, but once you step aboard a 40-plus-foot (13 meter) cruising catamaran crewed by family or friends in often lumpy conditions—well, things can seem a bit daunting. Especially when the weather forecast is in an unfamiliar language or dialect, delivered via a crackling radio.

We're here to help. We've spent years in the Caribbean—teaching sailing, running charter yachts—and we know that our experience could be of benefit. We aim to share our knowledge and a few tricks we've picked up about the region and its inhabitants—and to have you confidently guiding a modern cruising catamaran around some of the most beautiful and accessible cruising grounds the world has to offer.

Now, bareboating Caribbean style doesn't have to mean casually cruising with a *Red Stripe* in one hand while steering with a sunburnt foot. Rather, it means piloting a well-appointed yacht in close-to-ideal conditions without the issues that often plague higher latitude sailors—unpredictable weather, chilly temperatures, foul-weather gear, fog, big tidal ranges, and strong currents. At least not all the time.

YACHTS in the world's charter fleets have become increasingly sophisticated in recent years. They boast comfort, style, and more intricate systems. Virtually every model comes standard with a high capacity generator, air conditioning, electric freshwater heads/toilets, sound systems with speakers in multiple locations, and a reliable Wi-Fi connection. Some larger models might even include a watermaker and other amenities.

This sophistication brings with it a greater convenience but it can also bring greater complication and confusion. Electrical systems can always misbehave, generators can quit in the middle of the night.

> **NOTE**: *Murphy's great law prevails: If it can, it will. Break down, that is. (Though hopefully not on your charter!).*

Fortunately, along with the sophistication of the yachts there has been a related improvement in customer service—help is but a (free) phone call away.

Boat operation is as much an art as a science. There is rarely just one correct way to do anything on a boat, bareboat or otherwise. Whether it be docking, anchoring, battling head winds and swells or running before a storm, there is almost always more than one way of doing it.

So, if you have a technique that works and that won't break or scratch anything—or raise your blood pressure (or that of anyone around you)—stay with it.

We hope our guide will add to your body of knowledge and perhaps offer a fresh perspective on some of the familiar aspects of the Skipper's skill set.

Research and planning are key to any successful voyage. One excellent source for information on the popular islands is the message board, traveltalkonline.com

If you're new to the area you wish to charter, go on this site a few weeks or months prior and scan the archives—you'll get some relevant information from fellow charterers or year-round residents.

ANOTHER GOOD SOURCE is Noonsite.com which has extensive information on the cruising grounds of the Caribbean—and the rest of the world, too. It is especially useful for information on Customs and Immigration requirements. In addition, many of the specific islands have related social media groups for cruisers and visitors which are worth exploring.

THERE ARE, of course, many apps for phone and tablet that cover the Caribbean. The ActiveCaptain app is one we like, particularly if your charter yacht has a Garmin chartplotter or Navionics e-charts —your charter company representative may be able to tell you.

If you're sailing in the Virgin Islands, check out Simon and Nancy Scott's Cruising Guide the classic reference. If further down-island, get a copy of the Doyle Cruising Guide for the region you'll be in.

This excellent, long-established publication has a useful website with links to many amenities, such as a list of Facebook groups for just about every island in the region. Doyleguides.com

---

NOTE: *Check our website at SmarterCharterguides.com for links to sources for provisioning, immigration, navigation and other important information. These links are also available as QR Codes at the end of this book. These codes can be read by iPhone and iPad devices and may require a dedicated reader for Android phones and tablets (from the Play Store).*

ALSO, the individual charter company websites have a wealth of suggestions for the destinations they serve. By scanning them all you can get a comprehensive idea of the options and attractions available throughout the Caribbean.

3

The Charter Business
FUN IN THE SUN

The charter yacht trade has many homes—Greece and the Aegean, the Mediterranean, the Adriatic, Thailand, Mauritius, Tonga, Tahiti, The Great Barrier Reef, The Bay of Islands, Baja California, the Pacific Northwest and many more.

But nowhere is there such a variety of available boats coupled with ease of access as the Caribbean.

Just a few hours' flight-time from the US and Canada, with Peru, Chile, Argentina, and Brazil within a comparable radius of distance, there are thousands of modern yachts in comfortable anchorages in countries with familiar facilities and modern supermarkets, more or less. Flights from Europe make non-stop journeys to Antigua, Martinique, Guadeloupe, Puerto Rico, St. Lucia, St Martin, the Virgin Islands and other points.

THE COUNTRIES and territories of the Caribbean are generally relaxed when it comes to the certification and qualifications of skippers and crew. Unlike Europe, where 21 countries request an

International Certificate of Competence, the authorities of the Caribbean have few specific requirements.

The charter companies themselves, of course, do—as well as requiring an in-depth resume and often a checkout sail with an in-house professional, who has authority to suggest you take a skipper with you. Some companies are stricter than others—a trait that favors the consumer in that the stricter companies tend to have the less-abused and better-maintained boats. Most require a comprehensive sailing resume for the designated skipper and, on larger boats, at least one other member of the party.

THE MAIN DIFFERENCES among the charter grounds of the Caribbean lie in the convenience of travel, ease of shopping, and the distances that have to be covered when getting from one anchorage to the other. It's no surprise that the busiest charter grounds in the region—the British Virgin Islands—are a short distance from mainland USA, deal in US dollars as their official currency, speak English and are very stable politically.

Not only that, they are laid out in such a way that a chain of small islands on the south-eastern edge provides protection from waves from that quarter, while the larger islands provide a great degree of shelter from the storm-generated swells emanating off the North Atlantic. The resulting relative calm in the main channel of the chain, the Sir Francis Drake Channel, explains its colloquial name, *Drake Lake*.

> **NOTE**: *As we write, several of the larger BVI-based companies are offering to begin charters in St. Thomas in the USVI, hedging their Pandemic bets— an offer that may outlive the current crisis.*

WHILE RECENT AND ongoing events may have changed conditions somewhat, developments announced by major charter companies suggest new cruising grounds, from Cuba to Grenada, are opening up. Currently, Dream Yacht Charters offers a base in Cuba and another in Puerto Rico and the US Virgin Islands . Others, such as The Moorings, Sunsail, Horizon and more are branching out there and elsewhere.

Airports are being expanded, too, as islands compete more fiercely for the tourist and leisure traveler. And even without airport construction and expansion, new participants continue to join the market. Until recently, direct flights from New York/Newark, Miami, and other US and Canadian cities to over a dozen sailing destinations all over the Caribbean have been the norm, and should continue.

EAST FROM THE BVI, the cruising grounds of St. Martin lie exposed to the swells rolling in from the North Atlantic and Africa. Farther south, the Grenadines and other islands present challenges in the distances a boat has to sail to get from one anchorage to another—though those difficulties are offset by the relative lack of other cruisers, making these islands almost at times a private playground.

Many sailors begin their Caribbean chartering career in the welcoming waters of the BVI before venturing further down the Antilles chain. The options available will suit every preference—some destinations have direct flights from Europe and the US, some are a bit harder to reach—while the sailing becomes a little more challenging. As you venture east and south, facilities become less dependable and sailors are obliged to fend for themselves to a greater degree—which is not necessarily a bad thing.

MOST OF THE charter companies cited above either began in or maintain a major presence in the BVI and most of these also have bases further down the islands. St. Vincent, Grenada, Guadeloupe, Martinique, Antigua and Barbuda, St Martin and its neighboring islands—as well as those destinations already mentioned—are well served by the major companies and some local ones as well. These destinations are, in the main, well served by air transport, too— either directly or with a stop along the way. There is room for the sailor who wants to charter a boat for day sails whilst staying overnight in a villa by the beach as well as the family looking to cover some ocean miles.

———

WE KNOW a family from Germany who came regularly for over a decade and sailed from the BVI to Grenada and then island-hopped all the way back up to Tortola again. This 6-week odyssey filled their souls and gave them memories to cherish for a lifetime—or at least to hold them until they could come back two years later. They stopped only when the kids' progress from school to new careers made it impossible.

The Caribbean is a sailor's playground, able to indulge all manner of bareboating adventurers with options fitting every level of expertise and experience. So, when choosing a charter company, consider whether they offer discounts for future charters and other inducements, loyalty programs and the like.

You can also negotiate for better prices at different times—or if no shift on the pricing, the company might offer you an extra day or a night's pre-boarding or a free kayak. It's always worth trying, though the newest boats are usually in solid demand and not subject to discount. Ask where the best deals might be—maybe one of the other islands is doing less business than projected and is priced accordingly.

On the other hand, it might be in your interest to pay a little extra to cement a relationship with a top charter company. As competition increases, incentives will surely follow—and loyalty be rewarded.

But while changes are inevitable, and the near future still uncertain, the charter business has been and should long remain a strong pillar of local economies. Each year the boats get more comfortable, the amenities more varied, access more efficient, destinations more welcoming.

The great secret of yacht charter is that it has many price points from the top tier to the relatively inexpensive, but once you're on the water the fun is the same and the experience, well, priceless.

4

Prep Talk
GETTING READY

W hether this is your first charter or just one among many, there are always new elements to consider. If it's purely a family trip, the needs and preferences of all the participants will be fairly well established--there may be an allergy to manage, a medical condition to treat, an athletic routine that puts conditions on the charter. Does someone need to run for an hour every day? Practice yoga? Some of these requirements might narrow the list of destinations available to the group.

Has everyone been on a boat trip before? Is this the first trip to a particular part of the world, or a specific area of the Caribbean? Give everyone ample time to research the destination—or if the destination hasn't been finalized, let them weigh the options and offer their preferences.

IF YOU CAN MANAGE IT, try to be on charter around the time of Full Moon. Many areas celebrate the moon with dance parties and jump-ups. This involves research—choosing a destination—as well as chart work and close reading of the cruising guides. Some spots might require an early arrival in order to secure a mooring or better anchoring position.

And, unless you are a fan of sailing regattas, you might want to avoid Antigua during Sailing Week, the BVI during the Spring Regatta, Sint Maarten during the Heineken Regatta—which all follow one another pretty closely at the beginning of Spring. The waterways can be busy--and the marinas full.

> **NOTE**: *Given present conditions, health protocols may put a damper on these long-established events—but not for long (we hope).*

BEFORE COMING ON CHARTER, there are some essential tasks that need to be tackled. If some of the crew are not well known to each other, now is the time to develop crew cohesion. The Skipper—and there may be more than one, of course, perhaps sharing the responsibility—can put different members of the party together to do research, to practice techniques, to get themselves into the adventure mindset.

Set up a private group for all participants on social media. Or just a simple email group will suffice. That way people can share photos, web sites, articles, instructional videos and other relevant information. And get the family and friends thinking about the part they will play in the day-to-day operation of the yacht.. Maybe have a ZOOM-style meeting or Messenger/What's App chat to get to know one another, if that's an issue.

CREW ASSIGNMENTS:

Here are some ways to involve your crew in the pre-charter prep:

- Have the crew check the charter company web site to confirm what items are included on the boat and what are optional extras—toys (such as Stand Up Paddleboards), floating toys (inflatable flamingos), Wi-Fi, safety netting (for young children), hammocks and the like.

- If the information is not available, send an email. If possible, get a contact name at the base you are going to for on-the-ground information.

NOTE: *When requesting information, make sure there is only one point of contact from your crew. Multiple queries from different individuals at your end about the same charter can lead to confusion at both ends.*

- Ask for provisioning information, such as which companies deliver direct to the boat. Check the web forums, as already mentioned

- Request an inventory list by way of towels, soap/shampoo and galley cleaning items, garbage bags, and insect spray that come with the boat. Some charter operators provide a starter pack to cover you for the first couple of days, others don't provide anything in that department at all.

- Explore options for rendezvous dives or lessons, eco-tours, and other high-demand frolics. Be cautious about making commitments far in advance, since weather and other factors might dictate last-minute itinerary changes that make it difficult to keep appointments. Aside from some dates in the High Season you can most often book a dive or other activity when you arrive for your charter—or the week prior to your arrival—and are better able to make an informed decision on weather and itinerary.

- Browse web sites to see what events might be upcoming at your destination—Full Moon parties, national holidays, Mardi Gras, Carnival, New Year's. French islands have their special days, as do the Dutch, British, and US territories.

- Most Important—practice knots! The most useful preparation crew can make is to master these basic knots— the Reef Knot/Square Knot, Bowline, Clove Hitch, Cleat

Hitch, Round Turn and Two Half Hitches, Figure 8/Stopper Knot, Sheet Bend, Cow Hitch, and Rolling Hitch. You'll need these knots to attach mooring lines, brace the dinghy, secure paddle boards and dive tanks. To tie up to a dock. To attach fenders to a railing or lifeline. Consider having a knot-tying session weeks before the charter so everyone can practice—make a game of it! It is, however, a safety issue—you want to know your fellow sailors can secure a knot without too much hesitation. Try this link for examples.

- Make Passage Plans: These are options for each day's journey (with choices for those days when you decide to do nothing but loll on the beach or snorkel the reefs). These can be done way ahead of time and can be multiple choice. That is, make rudimentary passage plans with options should there be a large swell or intense wind gusts. Basically, which way do you turn as you leave your anchorage? (Check our Safety Pack for a sample).

- And if conditions change during the day, do you have an alternative? It's all very well to improvise when the destinations are just 15 minutes apart, but in areas where you have to sail—or motor—for an hour or more, it's good to have a Plan B.

- Also, when making passage plans, be modest about your daily mileage—at least in the beginning. An hour on the water can be more than enough for tender tummies after a long flight. Maybe try a quick jaunt to a nearby beach for a swim and lunch before heading to your first overnight destination. Though be prepared to stay at your first anchorage, especially if you have young kids aboard.

- Contact the charter company to learn what brand of chart plotter your catamaran is equipped with. There will likely be an app that you can download to your phone or tablet and link directly to it. Most company web sites have a link for such queries.

- Assign positions to your crew based on their expertise and experience—helmsman, navigator—and let them do their research. Younger crew can perform wonders as lookouts, fender monitors, water-toy wranglers and the like.

Personal Equipment:

Consider your clothing options: people often bring far too much. T-shirts (or equivalent), shorts, and sandals or flip-flops are the general rule though you might want to dress a bit for a night out. You can always bolster your supply of beachwear at many of the bars, restaurants, and boutiques along the way.

One complication is that if you leave home in winter, you'll need warm clothing for the beginning and ending segments—which you may be able to leave at the charter base rather than bring onboard. Also, the seating position on some catamarans is quite high above the water and there may not be a lot of shelter, so bring something warm and waterproof to wear when underway. The boat may have wrap-around Eisenglass-style curtains which have to be rolled up to survive a blustery day's breeze.

- Rash guards and swimming tops (for protection against sun, and stings and scrapes when around coral), snorkels and masks that fit properly (kid-sized ones particularly)-- though the boat will come equipped with a variety of sizes. If you are chartering in the winter season, prepare for some (relatively) chilly evenings. And everyone should have a wide-brimmed hat with a lanyard for sun protection.
- Luggage is a sensitive issue. Storage is at a minimum aboard the boat though you might be able to store empty suitcases—or ones stuffed with your winter gear—at the charter base while you are on the water. Soft luggage like a duffel bag is preferred for the boat since it can be rolled up and stowed under the bunk. Also, the farther afield you go—and the more flights you have to take—the more

likely that a bag could go missing, so pack as lightly as possible.

- Check with your doctor for all your medications—you may need to renew prescriptions. *Bring medications in their original containers and have copies of all prescriptions,* since authorities have been known to request them. Pack meds in your carry-on bag, not checked luggage, in case it goes temporarily missing during multi-leg flight transfers.
- Bring seasickness remedies. Scopolamine trans-dermal patches are highly effective (but not for everyone).
- Make sure all documents are up to date—passports, driving licenses, boating resume/dive certifications, etc. Do you need visas? Let your credit card company know your plans —even if they say you don't have to—since the Caribbean is a bit of a trigger for the banks. They may send a verification text or a phone call that you are unable to access, requesting a response before they release funds.
- See if your phone plan includes the country you'll be in— otherwise roaming will suck up money. Ask to have it added and make sure it covers data as well as voice calls! And get the details on the Wi-Fi service the charter company provides. It may be easier to use apps rather than the phone system.

Gear to Bring:

- Hand-held VHF radio. These days, almost all the islands have reliable mobile service and most smartphones work here, so many sailors use an app like WhatsApp as a messaging system. But as a safety measure and as backup, bring a handheld VHF if you have one. They work well should the Cellular network go down. All the better if yours has a GPS built in.
- Hand-held GPS, with spare batteries or charger, likewise.

For when the main chart plotter goes down (in an electrical storm for instance). You may not need it—but when you do, you really do. Mobile devices generally have a GPS capability—but make sure yours can work independently of Internet/data connection, since that can be unreliable.

- Some short (10 foot) length of thin but strong line, Spectra for preference. Your bareboat won't have many spare short lengths of strong line, which is handy for a multitude of jobs from securing the dinghy fuel tank to keeping the Stand Up Paddleboard (SUP) attached to the boat. Leave it behind when you finish charter.
- Cable ties in assorted colors to mark the anchor chain and other items. They needn't be very long—medium sized, or differing sizes. They can be useful for many purposes.
- LED headlamp for BBQ duty, night-time anchor inspection (with a red-light option), dinghy operation, and a host of other uses, such as reading in the cockpit after dark.
- Mini flashlights—with appropriate batteries.
- Basic first-aid kit with anti-bacterial cream, your preferred pain relievers, sun cream (SPF 30 is sufficient—but make sure it is reef-safe), top-level sticking plasters (*Band-Aid* type), and any other favorite brands. Most places in the Caribbean carry US brands along with French, Dutch, and British—depending on where you are.
- A selection of multi-sized zip-lock style bags. They are good for bagging sunscreen, toothpaste, meal leftovers and other messy stuff as well as wet items such as bathing suits; and documents, electronics, and other sensitive items.
- A good underwater camera—because you can't take your phone everywhere.
- Hammock (the netting type, without crossbars) plus attaching straps to rig between support structures on the boat's hardtop or transversely across the stern area. Some smaller ones can be rigged in the cockpit area for storing fruit such as oranges and bananas and/or dive masks, etc.

And you can tie a hammock between palm trees ashore (just watch out for the falling coconuts!)

- Insulated drinking water bottles. The islands have become very conscious of the environmental costs of plastic and other garbage. (Some charters now appoint a Recycling Officer to monitor plastic bags etc. These look like jelly fish in the water and can be fatal to turtles).
- Sharpie-style marker pens and masking tape to ID items such as water bottles, can and bottle tops for quick identification in a fridge or cooler. Also bring white electrical tape—*not duct tape*—to mark switches controlling dinghy lifts, the anchor windlass, and other items.
- Notebook (for chart briefing, boat briefing, etc.) Also for reference to questions raised by crew during preparation. These notes of course can be kept on a tablet or phone.
- *Speedo*-type swim goggles for use when operating the boat or the dinghy during rain squalls. Ski goggles (mask-type) will work even better. These are good because the nose is free— unlike with a dive mask where the nose is covered by the body of the mask and creates fog.
- Dry Bag: if you want to go ashore by paddle board—or swim to that famous bar that won't let you dinghy over.

MONEY MATTERS:

- Bring plenty of cash. Not every island has efficient communications, even at the best of times—making credit card payments unreliable. Phone connections can go down, internet traffic can be awfully slow. In addition, banks may charge extra fees for the Caribbean, making it expensive for the business owner, so they insist on a high minimum amount for credit card charges or impose a fee for the service. Cash is king. In many places the US dollar is easily accepted, even in Euro areas.

- Should you tip? Yes. Who? Everyone that does you a service. At the dock, in the bar, on the dive boat, in the taxi, everywhere. It doesn't have to be much, but think about how the day might have gone if there was nobody on the dock to catch your lines, to tell you how far to go forward, how close you are to the dock. You might still be there, going forward, going back, oops, forward again without the dock guy saying, 'Hey Cap, easy on the port engine, mon! Come forward now. Easy, easy. That's it!'

It's worth a few bucks.

DRESS TO DE-STRESS:

All the following should fit into a single soft duffel-type bag.

First question: Shoes/ no shoes?

Answer: It depends. Many sailors prefer to go barefoot on the boat. Which is fine until you stub a toe on a deck fitting or slip on a wet cabin sole. If you do choose to wear shoes onboard, they must have a light-colored sole. They needn't be fancy $100 nautical jobs—grab a $20 pair from the Big Box store or the supermarket. They only need to last a week—leave them behind for the dock guys. Never wear them off the boat—they'll just bring sand and dirt aboard. A slip-on type rather than a lace-up is best. So long as they have a decent grip they'll do. When off the boat, you'll be wearing flip-flops. If you prefer to wear shoes, bring a second pair for shore-side. You could always go for the Croc-type clog (though not everyone approves). They are low-maintenance though.

Mostly, whether male or female (or any variety thereof) you'll be living in shorts and t-shirts or your swimsuit. If you're missing an item, there are plenty of shops eager to sell you a shirt, shorts, hat, whatever. Bring the basics:

- 2-3 pairs of decent quick-dry shorts.
- The days of dressing formally for dinner (as some resorts used to require) are long gone. But some may want to spruce up a bit with a clean polo, or a crisp button-down, a fancy top.
- 1 T-shirt/top per day minimum (buy any extras at the many bars and restaurants)
- 2 shirts (with long sleeves preferably. Quick-dry, SPF-30+). For sailing and general outdoors work the Columbia/Patagonia/Gill styles work well.
- Plenty of underpants
- 2 swim suits
- 1 sweater or hoodie (for cool evenings). A sarong or wrap is extremely versatile—it can double as a beach towel.
- 1 lightweight waterproof jacket—preferably Gore-Tex
- At least one pair polarized sunglasses (plus safety/retainer cord)
- 1 good protective hat
- Sunscreen (SPF 30) + moisturizer. SPF-30 is all you'll need since you'll be swimming a lot and re-applying several times a day.
- Medications (as mentioned previously, bring a copy of any prescriptions).

NOTE: *If taking multiple flights, bring a carry-on bag with a change of clothes (T-shirt and shorts plus hoodie), swimsuit, and toiletry items, etc. for a couple of days.* Make sure you pack any needed medications (along with a copy of prescriptions). *The more changes you make en route the greater the likelihood your luggage will not arrive at the same time as you.*

5

Provisioning

DELIVERY OPTIONS

N o matter which island destination you choose, or which charter company, your arrival at the charter base will almost inevitably turn into a confusion of conflicting priorities and last-minute adjustments. Not only might you be exhausted from the travel, but there will be briefings to attend, supplies to purchase and stow, crew to instruct—among other things.

One time-saver is to pre-order provisions. Many of the islands have supermarkets or specialist vendors that offer this service—or the charter company might provide an in-house service. And, although it might seem tempting to simply pre-order everything and have it available when you arrive, what happens if your flight is delayed or your boat isn't ready? Do you really want your pricey perishables sitting in the hot sun for hours? (Some charter companies have devised systems to accommodate even this circumstance—ask if yours is one).

PERHAPS HOLD off on the perishables, but do get your packaged, canned, and bottled items—especially jugs of water—delivered. Having the heavy stuff dropped off leaves you free to shop around for meat, seafood, fruit, vegetables, cheeses, and other delicate items. Your charter company should be able to provide links to local stores that'll deliver direct to your boat. And most larger islands can accommodate diets of the gluten-free or vegan variety these days.

The taxi drivers know the drill. They'll wait for you or set a time to pick you up.

Most large supermarkets will have a taxi-driver waiting outside for customers—or the taxi that brought you from the charter base will arrange to come back in 45 minutes or so (but get the driver's name and phone number!)

It's tempting to think of finding wonderful fresh produce and fruit picked just days before on an island farm but it's hardly ever going to happen. Most provisions come in big containers from Miami twice a week. The French islands seem to have delicacies such as raspberries flown in on the last flight from Paris every day...but that might just be a fantasy! (Although many of these islands will provide you with fresh baguettes twice a day.) Ask your charter company if there are any local fresh food growers or markets.

The BVI's Aragorn Dick-Read supplies organically grown local herbs and vegetables from his Good Moon Farm, and can deliver by arrangement.

The storms of recent years have disrupted much of the islands' agriculture, so be sure and check with your charter company for the equivalent service in the area in which you're chartering—or check the message boards and social media apps online.

It helps to have a good idea of what you'll need for the duration of the trip. Charter chef Deb Mahan gave us these tips:

- Create a basic spreadsheet with a menu plan for each day. Working from that, you can be precise about the amount of vegetables, starches, and proteins that you will need.
- Count how many chicken breasts, how many rashers of bacon, the number of eggs and so on.
- As storage space is limited and refrigeration not always reliable, plan to eat the more perishable items earlier in the charter.
- Start your shopping list with items required for the first meal of the day through to dinners. As you think of an item, group it into proteins, fruit and vegetables, dry goods, and grocery items. You can then pick out non-perishable items that you can pre-order ahead of arrival, making your personal shopping much easier.
- Plan your itinerary to include a stop with a supermarket or decent grocery halfway through your trip.
- Have a meal ashore at a recommended restaurant every second day or so to give the chefs a break—and to make the provisions last a bit longer. And, hey, because you're on vacation!
- Download and print a copy of Deb Mahan'sMeal Planner spreadsheet—it's full of great ideas.
- And ask about genuine local producers for a taste of fresh locally grown fruits and vegetables. In several Caribbean islands there are farmers and purveyors of indigenous fruit

and veg. You'll find links to many of the sources throughout the islands on our web site.

- Some destinations will permit you to bring special foods such as frozen meats or seafood with you, packed in dry ice or just stacked while frozen inside a good travel cooler, such as a Yeti. Check with your airline!

6

Kids On Board

Yacht design has changed substantially in recent years. Where once a private yacht might be maximized for dealing with ocean conditions—big seas, strong winds—the newer versions are designed for socializing and time spent on anchor or at the dock. The tight interiors with built-in handrails and benchtops with raised fiddles have given way to sleek Corian-style worktops with little to hang onto should the need arise. But rarely does the need arise.

The wide-open interior spaces and deck areas of the catamaran do offer challenges for young children, so take extra care in both choosing the boat and in operating the one you've chosen. All boats will slam into an oncoming wave or lurch down the back of one that's just passed, possibly leaving the little ones sliding about—if they aren't properly supervised. Catamarans will bounce around quickly and, because of their greater speed potential, can throw crew in unexpected directions. And an oncoming swell, wave, or a large wake can stop them quickly too! The twin hulls can trap the wave, which might then slam into the bridge deck and make a bit of noise but won't usually cause any harm.

If you have small children on board, the charter company may be able to attach netting around the perimeter of the boat. The small fee is nothing compared to the peace of mind such protection will induce.

Regardless of age, you must have life jackets (PFDs) that fit your children. Specify the sizes you need ahead of your arrival and check that they are aboard when you get there. For kids under 6, some charter companies recommend bringing theirs with you if possible.

Do the same with dive masks: if the kids have one at home, pack it in the luggage—that way they won't have to endure an oversized, leaky mask. During high season, choice may be restricted at the charter base. If your kids are small, bring small swim fins too, if possible. These are items that not all charter companies are able to provide—though they might have commercial partners, such as dive shops, who can supply them to you if needed. Or check in a big-box store at your local mall—they often have kid-size gear for prices you won't find in the Caribbean.

Bring kid-sized gear if you have it.

Older kids (over 10, say) can easily get involved in the operation of the boat. There are many things they can do—sort out swim fins and masks, check that SUPs and kayaks are firmly attached to the railings, monitor the dinghy in its davits or when being towed, and even operate it if they fit the criteria laid down by the charter company (usually, over 16).

They can sweep out the saloon and help with garbage and other tasks that are essential every day, such as clearing laundry off the railings prior to getting underway and looking for loose items that might blow away. Give the older kids the responsibility for checking bilges, emptying holding tanks, checking engine oil and generally making themselves useful. And they make great lookouts!

One way to do it is to create a schedule and break the kids into teams so they can alternate duties. Teams can be assigned deck duty (tidying up loose items, securing SUPs, gathering up towels, etc.), saloon duty (washing dishes, putting things away that might fly around the saloon when underway, tidying up toys and card games, separating recyclables, etc.) plumbing duty (checking bilge float switches are clear of obstruction, prepping the holding tanks for emptying when underway in open water, etc.) and any other daily tasks that need attending.

———

BVI CHARTER CAPTAIN AND INSTRUCTOR, Donna Smith Acquaro, says, 'Kids love to learn new stuff. I recommend encouraging children to learn along the way. Bring books with the flora and fauna of the area—you can often find them at the charter base. Also, drawing materials and shock- and water-proof cameras.'

- And look at what your charter company (or local third-party vendor) offers in the way of water toys. These are age-dependent but range from swim noodles to kayaks and SUPs. Also take a look at your local drug store or mall outlets—they often have kid-sized inflatable toys and the like at ridiculous prices. Many folks bring these toys and leave them on the boat when they're done.

- Parents often bemoan the fact that kids on a boat seem to want to spend time texting, TikToking, or playing Minecraft on an iPad, rather than enjoying the gorgeous azure waters. But we have found that it pays to indulge the young set initially. The boat is an unfamiliar environment —often much friendlier to adult preferences than youthful ones. In a day or two the kids ought to relax and adapt. If not, it's easy to distract them with trips ashore. In most island destinations there are often stops along the way with kid-friendly food, and sand beneath the feet.
- A little family hiking trip can change the atmosphere immediately. Many restaurants offer kid-friendly entertainment, such as pirate shows and sing-alongs and for older kids there are surf clinics and kiteboard lessons.
- Or take a taxi tour of the island—you'll learn a lot of the history and culture, as well as find a great restaurant along the way. Ask at your orientation/chart briefing if they recommend any child-oriented shore stops.
- Some island anchorages feature amenities such as inflatable climbing walls, safe and easy snorkeling areas, even sandpits and playpens—aka the beach. Older kids (parents too) might enjoy hiking to the top of the island on dedicated trails to take in the view. Some areas feature horse and pony riding and other activities to suit various ages.

If all else fails, you'll at least have the onboard Wi-Fi to conjure up some silly videos—just don't check the news.

7

The Chart Briefing

This briefing is an essential element of the bareboat charter. While it is very rarely brief and it's not merely about the chart, it is crucial that the skipper and at least one other crew member attend. If time permits, and the crew are interested, bring them all.

> **NOTE**: *In this time of contagion, charter companies might restrict the briefing to just one crew member and insist upon some form of Social Distancing.*

Most charter companies offer a group briefing for all outgoing charters, either in the early evening the day prior to charter, or the morning of the first day—often both. You'll learn about the area and the environment in detail, as well as current events both cultural and meteorological. It can be overwhelming, so be sure to take notes for later reference.

This is an important resource even if you've sailed in the area before —things change all the time and memory is not a reliable navigational instrument! If some of your crew arrive late, have them sit-in on the next available briefing. That way you'll all be on the same page.

NOTE: *Memory is not a reliable navigational instrument. Take notes.*

If you hope to get out of the base quickly, the remaining crew could be going through the ship's inventory, stowing provisions, doing any last-minute shopping or sorting swim fins, topping off water tanks and all the other sundry tasks that remain undone. The following are among the topics covered in the chart briefing—and be sure to ask if something you are concerned about isn't specifically addressed:

- How to get a local weather forecast and where to get updates via VHF or local radio each morning or evening.
- Swell warnings and projected weather events.
- Any recent biohazards that have been reported (jellyfish during summer months, fly outbreaks, Sargassum seaweed beachings).
- Local dos and don'ts—dress codes, for instance. Some islands encourage a modest presentation.
- Current events that can impact your trip—you can encounter powerboat Poker Runs at various times of the year. These might affect your ability to anchor or find a mooring at a favored destination on a particular day. And they often take over the fuel docks for hours, so you aren't able to replenish diesel and water. Also there are various Full Moon parties and such that may require finding a mooring much earlier in the day than normal.
- A sample itinerary with the most popular stops described— as well as the No-Go areas, where your insurance coverage might be void.
- Communications protocols, such as phone numbers for assistance, etc.
- Procedures to follow on return from charter, such as fueling requirements.

- Hazards and/or local warnings—anything from a sunk boat or an exclusionary zone, to possible crime situations (in some locations, not all) such as dinghy theft hot spots.
- The types of Navigational Markers you'll encounter—such as Cardinal Buoys—and any missing markers, as well. Plus any special rules, off-limit areas, etc.
- Spring in the Caribbean is the time for high-level racing regattas—you can find yourself suddenly in the middle of a hard-charging fleet. Check with your briefer.
- At almost any time of the year, there are sailing club flotillas and other groups that, while fun to share a dance floor with ashore, can make finding a mooring somewhat challenging. Such groups won't all be leaving from the same charter base as you of course, so ask around.
- Try to obtain an itinerary from any such flotilla—just walk up to one of the participating boats on your dock (you'll know by the flags and banners flying from the topping lift) and ask. Customer Service personnel at the charter company should have an itinerary sheet at their disposal, too. Some areas are host to regattas put on by the sailing magazines and yacht clubs.
- So if you encounter any such group, try to get their itinerary—and either follow along or go the opposite direction!
- You can also ask the personnel on a crewed yacht if they know any information that could assist you. Usually they are only too happy to advise—they'd rather help out before you start the charter than have to come to the rescue when boats drag anchor at midnight in an unruly and crowded anchorage!
- Make a record of any changes to relevant phone numbers for things like medical clinics, emergency services, hospitals and the like. (These are generally listed in the onboard Briefing Manual, but the information may need updating.)
- The information you learn at the Chart Briefing can

impact the final version of your Passage Plan. So make sure you review any plans already written out.

- You may have written passage plans weeks before you arrive in the islands. If not, research tide heights and times, phases of the moon, particular events at different destinations. Write up a number of alternate plans and, depending on the weather patterns on the day of charter, you can choose which one to implement.

NOTE: *Tides have minimal effect in the Caribbean, but the resulting currents can affect entrances and narrow channels.*

ABOUT THOSE SWELLS:

From late October until late May, exactly corresponding to the busiest charter season, Caribbean islands can be subject to sudden changes to the near-shore sea state. These sudden changes have nothing to do with the local atmospheric conditions.

The ambient weather could be perfectly fine with sunny skies and moderate trade winds from the east to north-east with the usual wind-driven swells of around 3-4 feet (around one meter)—all perfectly normal in the West Indies. But two thousand miles away in the North Atlantic, autumnal and winter storms kick up big seas that, 2-3 days later, ripple their way south to the islands' warm and sunny shores.

Along the way, these large waves diminish in height and, because they're not all moving at exactly the same speed, catch up and merge with one another to form rows of fewer but more powerful waves. If you're flying down from the north-east part of North America on your way to the Caribbean you sometimes see them clearly if you're in a window seat.

In the ocean, this accumulated power is not manifest as higher waves but as longer-period waves: that is the time between each successive crest or trough of a wave gets longer, often around twice what the period was before they merged. When you leave coastal waters and sail truly offshore — blue water sailing— this is one of the big differences sailors notice, these longer period swells caused by distant storms.

The reason the coastal sailor doesn't usually experience this is that waves slow down as they encounter shallower water and they start to bunch-up to one another and get taller—often twice their deep water height. This effect of the seabed on the incoming waves creates what are known as 'ground swells' or 'ground seas'. Be fore-warned: the reason surfers flock to them is the very reason sailors should avoid them.

FOR CENTURIES, bays and harbors with good holding ground that offer some shelter from this E/NE quarter have provided safe overnight shelter for vessels. Whatever modest wave action is occurring outside the bay is blocked by a protruding headland or semi-exposed reef that reflects or absorbs the waves' energy.

But when the waves come from a direction different to the local wind—from the direction of those distant storms—these normally safe bays are left exposed and become uncomfortable and sometimes even dangerous to be in.

The best way to avoid them is to check not just the wind forecast and whether it's going to rain or not but to look at the wave forecast as well—and not just for the day ahead but especially for the evening ahead.

All the online forecast sites offer this and the dedicated surfer sites do an especially good job. But what you need to look out for are overnight changes to both the wave direction and its period.

A typical forecast showing changing swell direction

When waves shift (if only for a few hours) to the NW or N do not plan to overnight in north-facing bays. In fact, get away from north-facing coasts and seek shelter on the south sides of islands where at all possible (and in the Caribbean with so many islands to choose from, it's almost always possible). Call the charter company for advice if you're unsure. They know the islands and have access to all the local forecasts so they can either reassure you of your choice or give you a pointer to somewhere safer.

WHAT ARE the likely risks when stuck in a vulnerable anchorage after sunset?

1. Unless you're the boat's owner and experienced in piloting a boat in the dark off an unfamiliar, poorly lighted coast you're simply begging for trouble. Even then, should any accidental damage happen to your boat--or anything you hit--your insurance would be void because charter yachts are forbidden from being under way at night unless they have an explicit, written waiver from the charter company.
2. Going ashore in the dinghy in these conditions is out of the

question: if it didn't get swamped during an attempted beach landing, it would get swamped trying to get back out. Provided, that is, the dinghy survived being left unattended on the sand while everyone's at the restaurant. Even if there's a normally safe dinghy dock, the dink risks getting smashed, punctured, or jammed underneath it—an occasional risk in the BVI's Cane Garden Bay.

3. If it's not already too late, check the mooring bridle for chafe in places where it touches the boat **and be sure to have two, independent, bridles attached to the mooring pennant.** If anchored, deploy a second hook or, if space allows, let out more chain to help absorb the up-down motion of the swell.

Since you're on a catamaran consider yourself fortunate or smart in your selection. The cat's motion—particularly rolling—will be unpleasant but much, much less so than if you were on a monohull.

PREPARATIONS: Double-check that the boat is not going to drag its anchor or cut through its mooring bridle, secure any loose objects— doors, drawers etc.—and (carefully) prepare something to eat. Think sandwiches or other finger food rather than a proper meal. This is not the time to prepare a gourmet meal, as any loose items on the galley counter or on a table are likely to slide off. Be especially careful of sharp objects and glass bottles. Take care when opening overhead lockers in case heavy cans or plates tumble out on top of you.

HAVE AN EARLY NIGHT. Turn-in and try to get some sleep. If the conditions are still rolly-polly in the early morning, check the wind and wave forecast again, choose a safe haven as the next destination and motor out at first light--after making sure that any open port lights and hatches are closed. Pay particular heed to the channel markers (if any) as you exit.

Get well offshore—at least a mile—before turning parallel to the coast. That experience, while uncomfortable, should remain fresh in your mind when choosing overnight stops in the future!

8

The Boat Briefing

W hatever your level of experience, the Boat Briefing is an essential component of instruction before leaving the safety of the charter base. Charter company staff will lead the crew through the on-board equipment and operational procedures of the vessel. There is a lot of information to absorb—one way to deal with it is to delegate aspects to different crew members. Have one person specialize in the engine operation, another in anchoring systems etc.

NOTE: *The briefers have a sequence they follow. One piece of information leads to another, so try to hold questions until the briefer gets to that topic— once items get out of sequence, things can get skipped over or missed entirely.*

But don't hold back—if you are not confident you understand an item, ask for more information and make notes as you go.

ANCHOR BALL: Learn how to assemble and raise it in the boat's fore-triangle. Ask how best to secure the main halyard to stop it from wrapping around a spreader or slapping against the mast. Have the briefer supply you with a length of light line to secure it, if not already provided.

Autopilot: An invaluable item so long as you master its operation. Make sure that all crew learn the procedures, too. It's not unheard for the person at the helm to inadvertently hit the 'Engage/Auto' button and find they can no longer steer the boat—and not be sure why. Check that the Autopilot is disengaged when departing the dock, otherwise you might T-bone the boat across the way. When motoring long distances, the autopilot is often the preferred helmsman, but it must be monitored by crew. Ask whether your autopilot allows for Course or Wind settings and how to access these.

Mark the center point of the steering wheel with some electrical tape. Rotate the wheel from hard a-port to hard a-starboard and halve the number of turns. Wrap some tape at Top Dead Center. Crosscheck with the autopilot display.

Battery Charging: Make sure you get proper instruction in battery-charging procedures when running engines for that purpose. If you have questions, don't hesitate to ask the briefer.

> **NOTE:** *A fully charged 12-volt battery system should be taken to a level of 14.2-14.4 volts initially, if there is no drain on the system. Once the charger is disconnected, the voltage should fall to around 12.8 volts. Don't let it get any lower than 12 volts—and even that is too low a charge, about 25% of capacity.*

Ask how to properly monitor battery states of charge. Though you'll most likely have a generator on board which will take care of all charging needs when running, there may be a circumstance (generator failure) in which you need to charge the house batteries with one or other propulsion engine—or just quickly warm-up some water for hot showers or dishwashing.

Bilge Pumps: Make a basic map of their locations. Particularly ask to hear them in action. Get all crew familiar with the sound of an active bilge pump. It might indicate water dripping from an air conditioner condenser, or it might simply be a stuck float switch—one that needs to be poked with a broom handle or boat hook to reset—so know how many float switches there are and their locations.

Boat Papers: If you are planning on going to another jurisdiction —crossing from the BVI to the USVI or St. Martin, for example— make sure you have the requisite papers. The charter company needs to know well beforehand if you're planning such a trip, since it may affect the choice of vessel they supply to you—some individual boats may not fit the regulatory requirements.

Request customs forms, too. You'll need the boat's registration information and, when returning to the original port of departure you'll need a copy of your cruising permit. These are usually located in the chart table. Make sure there's a chart in there as well. And remember that when clearing in to a new port you'll be asked for your clearance from the previous one. Read the fine print closely, since some forms require many signatures, as well as addresses and other details for all passengers.

Chart Plotter: Probably the most important piece of equipment in the cockpit is the chart plotter/GPS. Take the time to understand the proper sequence for loading pages, entering information and saving waypoints and routes etc. Are the depths in feet or meters? How to engage/disengage alarms? Ask the briefer to locate the instruction manual for the equipment. Often it is buried under a seat cushion in the saloon somewhere. If you can't locate it, go online using the boat's Wi-Fi and download a copy from the manufacturer's web site.

Cockpit Lockers: Go through them thoroughly, since this is where you'll find emergency equipment, flares, PFDs etc. Also swim fins, masks, dive flag, and other useful gear. You may be able to organize lockers so as to stow some beverages and other bulky items.

Depth Gauge: Possibly the most important source of information in your multi-function chartplotter. Is it calibrated to read from the sea surface, from the transducer (about 1-2 feet below the surface), or from the bottom of the keel? Whichever it is, make sure you know how to calculate your true safe depth for operation. And if it's in meters and you'd prefer it in feet (or vice versa) ask your briefer to change it for you.

Dinghy Security: We get into dinghy procedures in a later chapter, but here we'll look at security aspects. The dinghy is a valuable asset—worth many thousands of dollars and of practical utility to almost everyone. They have been known to disappear off the dock and from the moored or anchored yacht—unless properly secured. On a catamaran, the dinghy will be hoist in davits. Make sure there's a length of line available so you can prevent the dinghy from swinging side-to-side when hoist. Ask the briefer to supply a length of light line for this if not already provided and to locate and demonstrate the security cable and lock for the dinghy. In some locations, the charter company may advise you to get into the habit of locking the dinghy to the mother ship every night.

Emergency Tiller: Where is the emergency tiller and how does it fit to the rudder stock? Ask the briefer to demonstrate how to use the cockpit winches to turn the tiller when the boat is underway (when water is flowing over the rudder, you won't be able to do so without some mechanical assistance). It doesn't happen every day, but boats lose their rudders – or more likely, bend the rudder post – more often than you'd think by hitting a whale, a rock, or floating debris. The latter is particularly common in the summer when tropical storms dump torrents of rain on the steep hillsides, washing fence posts and other hazards into the waters. If your catamaran has hydraulically actuated steering, you'll need to disengage that system to operate the emergency tiller. Make sure you ask the boat briefer how to do this.

Engine Operation: Go over everything from the correct starting procedure, to the fuel system, to emergency stop procedures. Some boats will have a key start but most now have electronic starts that require a sequence of switching. Make sure you understand it, since it's easy to turn off the ignition whilst the engine is still running. See where the fuel refill port is located (we know a group of bareboaters —on a monohull, however—who pumped the bilges full of diesel after mistaking the emergency tiller cap for the fuel intake).

> **NOTE**: *A good estimate of fuel consumption is around 1 US Gal/4 liters per hour for every 40HP/28Kw. Your generator would be about half that rate at full load.*

Entertainment Tech: Boats come with a variety of entertainment options from big-screen TV to multi-stage audio players with inputs for direct connectors, Bluetooth, and other technologies. In some cases you'll be able to direct-cast from your tablet or phone straight to a big screen or sound system, so ask for a full explanation. If you have a teenager onboard, they might be the best option for gaining rapid insight into the complexities of the system—or do an internet search of the stereo and download its manual to your phone to find out how to pair it

First Aid Kit: The kit supplied with the boat does not always have the best selection of treatment options. Someone is going to need it at some point since an insect bite, a stubbed toe, sunburn, even a jellyfish sting (or a hangover) are not outside the realms of possibility. Make sure it is fully stocked and have available the additions you brought with you—high quality Band-Aid type plasters, antihistamines, good pain relievers etc. Keep the kit in an easily accessible place and make sure everyone knows where it is.

Freshwater Pump: With the proliferation of fresh water toilets and en suite showers, you'll use more fresh water than you might otherwise expect.

> **Note**. The Universal Water Rule is: *Fresh water lasts in inverse proportion to the amount of hair on the boat.*

Usually you'll have to switch the manifold valve from one tank to the next. Crew should be familiar with the sound of the running water pump—it could mean either a leak, a tap left running, or it might indicate that the water tank is empty and the valve needs switching. It is often hard to hear the pump when the generator is running. The water pump can often run 'dry' but only for a short period—repeated dry runs day after day may burn out the pump. If the boat has a watermaker, you'll need to run it for at least a couple of hours every day. Get a thorough instruction in the intricacies of this equipment.

Do not have all the water-tank valves open at the same time.

Generator Operation: Master the proper sequence for starting and stopping it. Locate the reset button in case the generator quits —usually because of being overloaded—and won't produce any current after restarting. There is generally a push-button reset on a bulkhead panel next to the generator.

Locate the through-hull that feeds cooling water through the generator. You'll need to know which is the dedicated seacock/through-hull for the cooling water intake. This intake is liable to be blocked if there is much free-floating Sargasso-type seaweed around (generally in the summer), so learn how best to clear it.

ABOUT THE GENERATOR:

As much as the modern catamaran might resemble a smart apartment or condo, it does have some limitations. For example, a shower is a wondrous thing after a long day sailing in the tropical breeze— Interrupted by the occasional beach and snorkel excursion.

It's a chance to get rid of all that sunscreen and sticky sand. *Oops*...just kidding about the sand, which will have been rinsed from the body before arrival back on board the boat. Right? (We recommend everyone exit the dinghy by slipping into the sea a few meters from the boat and performing a sand-sluice prior to boarding).

Anyway, after the shower—including a shampoo and condition— those with flowing locks might be tempted to fire up the hair dryer.

Not so fast! Most so-called 'travel' hair dryers are rated at 1500W which, when loaded suddenly onto the average bareboat generator —which is already busy trying to cool down a hot boat full of hot people—will very likely cause the breaker to trip and shut the generator down completely.

If two people--or more--are simultaneously using hair dryers, that generator will certainly shut down. It's not the end of the world, but it's a drag to have to go through the proper start-up cycle and resetting of aircon units and other rituals.

There are solutions to the problem, of course:

1. Check the capacity of the generator--it may be able to handle the increased load.
2. If the genny is close to maxed out, shut down the aircon for a while. The boat will stay cool for the 30 minutes or so that are needed to complete the mission. Or,
3. If there's enough time and the trade winds are blowing steadily across the deck, find a suitably breezy spot--and a suitable beverage--and let those locks dry naturally.

INVENTORY: There should be an inventory list or manifest aboard the boat. Go through this thoroughly with the briefer. For two reasons:

1. you'll be charged for items not on the boat when you return and,
2. most important, it's the best way of learning where everything is.

Propellers and Rudders: Find out if you've got right- or left-handed props, a Sail Drive or fixed shaft. Should the propeller be allowed to rotate freely when under sail or should you engage reverse gear to stop it from spinning?

Reefing Lines: There should be at least two reefs pre-set in the main. Follow the lines aft and check the colors of the lines tied around the boom (reef #1 is always farthest aft) and follow them forward to verify that they are correctly labeled at their clutches.

Refrigeration: Check the location of the thermostat and that it is properly set. Some boat refrigerators get very cold and can freeze lettuces and other fragile vegetables—not to mention eggs and milk.

Running Rigging: Sort through the lines that run through blocks and sheaves. These lines are often color-coded, so ask for an explanation if you are uncertain. This category includes mainsheet, jib sheets, halyards, reefing lines, downhauls and outhauls—any moving lines.

Stack Pack: (Canvas cradle holding the classic mainsail). If it has a zipper along its top, unzip it before leaving the dock—and don't bother with it again until the end of your charter.

Stove Operation/Barbecue Grill: Nothing will drive you crazier than a stove that won't light or won't stay lit. Many stoves and ovens are self-lighting but we recommend you buy a long-barreled stove lighter—one that can reach all the way to the back of the oven. These units vary from boat to boat. Make sure you get a thorough training in how to light it and how to control temperature. By 'thorough' we mean have the briefer actually light it—not just point at the controls and give a verbal run-through. This is temperamental equipment—but crucial to the well-being of skipper and crew!

Toilets and Holding Tanks: The marine toilet is, other than the depth sounder, possibly the most important piece of equipment on the vessel! Pay close attention to the briefing, since a malfunction can have serious consequences. Many catamarans have the heads en-suite and thus have no central units available for general use, so if one toilet goes down, some crew will be obliged to share toilets/showers etc. Locate the holding-tank outlet valves. You will be using them pretty much every day, so either make sure the occupants of the relevant cabins learn how to work them, or delegate the task to a single crew member or on a rotating roster.

VHF Radio: Learn how to operate the unit and, if close to US territories, how to get a weather forecast by accessing the WX button--though not all VHF units have this capability. A surprising number of VHF units are set to the wrong channels or seem unable to receive signals. Make sure yours actually works properly by performing a radio check with the dockmaster prior to leaving the charter base, or by using your handheld unit. Know how to make a Mayday call. And make sure as many crew as possible get these lessons since, in a real emergency, some crew could be incapacitated or busy on other tasks.

Windlass and Anchor: Learn how to release the clutch by letting it freewheel for quicker anchor dropping. If you've brought some colored cable ties with you, attach them to the anchor cable at regular lengths (if the charter company hasn't done that already), beginning at 50 feet and every 50 feet after. Use any color system that makes sense to you. e.g. traffic light green for first 50' orange for next 50' and red for the next 50'. Most bareboats will have 50 metres of chain (around 164'). Anchor snubber line: where is it? How do you attach the hook? Remote control—are you sure you understand how it works?

NOTE: *How to allow sufficient time to get to your destination: When beating upwind—closehauled—the distance you actually sail through the water when compared with the rhumb line (straight line) distance from where you are to where you want to go will obviously be greater due to the zig-zag nature of sailing to windward. Very approximately, this will be around 1.4 times the run line for boats (and their crews) that tack though 90 degrees and around 1.7 times for boats that tack through 100 degrees—i.e. cruising catamarans...and poorly sailed cruising monohulls.*

AND THIS DOESN'T INCLUDE two other factors:

1. **Leeway**—the sideslipping that always makes sailboats 'crab' slightly sideways as they move forward. When you're sailing upwind, leeway is always sending you slightly downwind at the same time. How much depends on your keel and rudders' bite into the water, your heel angle (for a monohull), your speed and the sea state. While it could be 5 degrees in a well-sailed monohull, it could be 10 degrees or more in a poorly-sailed cat—especially in choppy water.
2. **Tidal current**—this could be a) with you, b) against you or c) across you. Even in the Caribbean where tides and their associated currents are much less than further away from the equator, it's normal to experience a northwest 'setting' (i.e. going northwest) oceanic current called the 'Equatorial Current'.

For a back-of-the-envelope safe calculation, figure that while your distance sailed through the water might be 1.5 times the straight line for a reasonably well-sailed monohull, it could be twice that for a cruising catamaran.

9

Head Mastery
GAME OF THRONES

Traditionally it's The Heads, or The Head, but let's be bold and call it the toilet. It's possibly the most important piece of equipment on the boat and is as sensitive as an opera star. Treat it like it's #1 and it won't behave like it's #2, OK?

> **NOTE**: *Nothing…NOTHING…should go down the toilet unless it's been through your digestive tract first.*

Well, maybe paper. Small pieces of paper. No wads, no fistfuls. Little pieces, a couple of sheets at a time. And flush between the sheets. No toenail clippings, razors, dental floss, hairclips, rings, tampons, watches, dentures—you name it, they've all been in there. So please keep all foreign objects out of the bowl. No baby wipes, 'flushable' or not. No hair from the hairbrush. No bits of fluff off your shirt. Nothing but little bits of TP.

THE REASON IS THAT, on most modern yachts, everything that goes into the toilet has to pass through a very small and weak blender/grinder called a macerator. If things get stuck in the macerator it can't do any macerating. You do not want to listen to your toilet attempting to digest a toothbrush. It's no fun. That means someone has to get down on hands and knees and disassemble the whole contraption and clean it out and reseal it, which often means unscrewing the toilet base from the floor of the bathroom and generally turning the Throne Room into the Poop Deck. Bad! It could be one of the crew.

Or, it will mean waiting for the chase boat to meet you the following day and attend to the problem. Either way it's a nuisance—one that's easily avoided.

MANY OF THE newer units flush with fresh water but most still use sea water. Except for the need to keep your water tanks topped up, there is no tangible difference as far as you are concerned, but in the long term the fresh water device is a better proposition—less corrosion, less odor.

Almost all the units you will encounter will be electrically filled and flushed via a rocker switch that pumps water into the bowl and drains the contents through a macerator and into a holding tank. The most common model of toilet also has a separate rinse rocker switch, which does what you imagine it does.

————————

THE PROPER WAY TO use the toilet is, after raising the lid:

- First, pump water into the bowl.
- Then sit down on the open seat. And Gentlemen, this includes you. Yes, sit, every time.
- Do your business, whatever form it might take.
- If necessary, wipe the sensitive parts of your body.
- Rather than flush the soiled sheets, place them in the bin. Baby wipes or paper towels go there as well—usually inside a sealable paper or plastic bag. Save plastic shopping bags for this purpose or bring/buy a box of small plastic bin liners. This way you reduce the risk of clogging the macerator.
- Flush away the evidence.
- If the evidence refuses to completely disappear, flush again. And again. Leave it as you'd like to find it.
- When all evidence has disappeared, press the rinse button and then pump out as much water as possible from the bowl so it doesn't slosh around and spill over when underway.
- Wash your hands.

NOTE: *Flush the bowl empty so there's little to no water in it. Close the seat at all times when not in use—things can fall into the toilet and really jam up the works. That includes baby wipes.*

THE GAME OF THRONES:

Your boat will come equipped with holding tanks that receive and store the black water from the toilets. When you're in bays and harbors—anywhere people are swimming around the boat—keep those tanks closed by shutting the valves that you were shown during your boat briefing. Empty the tanks daily or every-other-day. Do it when you are en route from one anchorage to the next and as far offshore as you're going to get. Include the evacuation of the holding tanks as part of your daily Passage Plan. And make sure you comply with local regulations regarding discharges—not in National Park areas, for example. And don't empty the tanks while operating the generator while anchored or on a mooring—you might suck the contents into the genny. Bad!

> **NOTE**: *While the valves need to be closed when you next enter an anchorage or marina, it is most important that you return to the base at the end of your charter with the valves draining the holding tanks in the OPEN position. If you return with full tanks, you will likely be assessed a fee.*

10

Island Hopping
CLEARING IN/OUT

The islands of the Caribbean are variously self-governing entities, such as Dominica, or overseas dependencies of large nations, such as the Virgin Islands (British or US). Some territories share the same island, such as St. Martin/Sint Maarten. The separate Saba and Statia are affiliated with the Kingdom of the Netherlands and thus the EU. Whenever you leave one jurisdiction and enter another you will be required to file paperwork with either one or both places. Some may require visas but all will require ship's papers, crew passports, their forms filled-in correctly and money—in their local currency.

None of the officers you meet and to whom you'll offer your documents is in any great hurry to rush the process. But don't be tempted to debate any of the requirements or betray too much impatience—you'll only delay the proceedings.

You may feel as if your presence deserves some kind of reward, since you are bringing your hard-earned money to spend in this little piece of Paradise. But to the officials, you are simply a person to whom they may or may not grant the privilege of entry. And it is a privilege, not a right. It's their Paradise, after all.

So be polite and patient and ask a few questions about the best places to see. And don't be in too much of a hurry. It is often to your advantage to begin every conversation with 'Good morning,' or 'Good afternoon,' in the local language as the first words of your first sentence—there is a formality to the discourse that can be quite endearing.

And, if you find the whole rigmarole just a little ridiculous, don't let on or you might find yourself at the back of the queue wondering what happened. Wait for the reply. Then you could ask something like, is there a restaurant featuring the island's specialties to advantage? Churches are often a fertile topic for conversation—ask if there's one of significance you might visit.

IF YOU ARE THINKING of taking your yacht to a different jurisdiction, the charter company needs to know from the outset. Some companies have restrictions on where you can take their vessels and they may need to supply you with extra paperwork such as the boat's original documentation, import permits, proof of insurance, or they may have to add some extra equipment.

Caribbean on one tack.

They'll know what's required and whether or not you need to clear out of the country before you leave. They may also need to supply you with a boat that can pass the requirements for entry to that jurisdiction.

Most charter companies will have the yellow Q flag on board but the courtesy flag for the country that you're visiting may not be included in the yacht's standard inventory. Check before you leave because not flying the correct courtesy flag (or flying it upside down) is, well, discourteous.

BEFORE YOU LEAVE the charter base, where you'll have access to a photocopier, make multiple copies of your crew manifest—names, addresses, passport number, and so forth—as some territories require as many as 3 or 4 copies and you may be visiting more than one foreign territory. A trip starting in St. Martin, for example, may also include Anguilla, Saba, and St. Barths—sometimes two in the same day.

WHEN YOU GET to where you're going, make sure that your former courtesy flag is down and exchanged for the yellow Q flag. While unlikely, if your passage took you into international waters, the former should have come down as you left territorial waters.

If you're just planning on staying a day or two then you can ask to clear in and out at the same time, so as to avoid having to come back and do more paperwork before you leave. Most islands allow you to stay 24-48 hours this way, though it varies.

Are the crew permitted to go ashore while the captain is clearing in the vessel? Some island territories are very strict, some are lax and most are reasonable. Check the boat's cruising guide (and websites such as Noonsite.com) for a list of the ports of entry and the exact location and opening hours of the government buildings you must visit.

ALSO, the time of year is important. If you arrive in, say, St. Barths, around New Year you will find it filled to the brim with superyachts and attendant crew, celebrities, and craziness. This is not the best time to present the Customs and Immigration authorities with complications. They are overwhelmed with sensitive issues already. Have all your documents ready, passports open, and a smile affixed. And money in the correct currency! Be prepared to wait. But show up six months later and you'll find the harbor empty, the officials relaxed, and you might even get a space right on the dock.

When going ashore, bring a waterproof bag for carrying documents and passports (it might be a wet dinghy ride to clear in). And don't forget a pen! You might need local currency (Euros, EC dollars, US dollars) to pay entry fees. Not everyone takes credit cards. Prepare for all eventualities.

And after you've cleared in with both Immigration and Customs, and before you wander out to explore the town or have a leisurely lunch, you should send someone back to your boat to take down the 'Q' flag and replace it with the courtesy flag of the country you've now legally entered. Though, if your stay in town is to be brief, it can wait until your return.

11

Ship's Chat
SIGNS + SIGNALS

Clear communications aboard ship are crucially important. Wind and engine noise can make it hard to communicate along the length of the vessel. Layouts differ between and among different makes and models of catamaran. Some have the driving position in a raised helm station to one side or the other—leaving sightlines obscured by the mast. Others have a central position in an elevated area directly behind the mast but with a less obstructed view. None have unobstructed views when close to objects such as a dock or nearby traffic.

So, when approaching a mooring or preparing to release the anchor, the operator can be at a disadvantage, since the closer the vessel gets to the mooring or drop point, the less visible the dock, mooring ball or the sea bed become.

The solution to this problem is to use a signal system that is simple, clear, and easily understood. Signals are best when uncomplicated, so practice them in the cockpit area before implementing them properly. The signal should be maintained for as long as the procedure is needed. With an occasional exception—for instance, keep the fist raised and clenched to signal for neutral, but then extend the arm out to indicate the direction to turn the boat.

Below are the signals we have found work the best:

SHOULD THE BOAT BE IN GEAR?

- *Neutral*: Clenched fist raised at ear height.
- *Forward*: Open vertical palm/tomahawk chop in direction of desired movement at ear height. Increase rate of hand movement to reflect desired speed.
- *Reverse*: A reverse wave of the hand with flat palm facing backwards OR a gentle pat on the buttocks—(it may sound silly but it's unambiguous and so it works. When you need reverse, you usually really need it!).

WHICH WAY TO STEER IN NEUTRAL?

- Extend arm and hand in the direction the boat needs to go.
- Direction to steer in neutral is the steady hand pointing the appropriate way—no chopping.

DISTANCE OFF DOCKS, NEARBY BOATS AND MOORING BALLS?

The best way for the driver to judge distance off a dock or other obstruction is to have crew stand somewhere within—but not blocking—the helm's field of view, with arms fully outstretched. The forward edge of the appropriate hull is usually the best when approaching bow first. If the boat is reversing, a crew member standing midships can relay the instructions from the crew member observing at the stern.

- Have them wait until the dock comes to the same distance as their fully outstretched arms (let's say that span is 5' 6" /168 cm) before beginning the procedure. Any distance more than that is not an issue.
- As you approach the dock, your crewmate brings their hands together to indicate the distance off. This visual representation is clear and precise and can be used when squeezing through a narrow gap in a marina or mooring field—as well as when approaching a mooring ball, or dropping anchor in the centre of a sandy patch between sea grass.
- Start the signals at one or two boat lengths off the target—more if there is a lot of traffic or heavy wind affecting progress—when approaching a mooring or anchor drop.
- When docking, the first signals may be describing direction and speed but may revert to Distance Off when close to the target. And when docking, the crewmember signalling may have to communicate direction, speed, and distance-off all at the same time!
- This person effectively has control of the boat—so sightlines must be clear. When docking, make sure the line handlers don't get in the line of sight. At the same time, the driver is responsible for overall safety and seamanlike decision-making. Right-of-way rules need to be observed at all times.

OTHER USES:

In all cases these signals are generally well understood:

- Palm of hand raised in the universal traffic cop gesture means: STOP.
- Thumb raised in universal OK shape means: Okay or Good.

NOTE: *Spend a few moments with the crew each day, particularly when you'll be docking or in a busy anchorage, making sure they understand the signals and when they should be used. Confusion can be costly.*

12

Local Knowledge
BOAT BOYS + OTHERS

Throughout the Caribbean, enterprising entrepreneurs—known everywhere as Boat Boys, though some are female—offer valuable services. Approaching your boat in mooring fields and anchorages (but not marinas) they will offer to sell you ice, take away garbage, and may display a range of provisions.

Sometimes they dawdle on their way and at others they may race against a competitor or two—it depends on the time of day and the season.

Before coming alongside they will usually ask if you want what they have and if you say, 'No thanks,' they'll just move on to the next boat. They will usually not harass you if you don't want what they're selling. There are times, though, when their technique is more insistent.

Whether offering assistance in guiding you to a mooring or displaying a cooler filled with fish, the Boat Boys are eager to close the deal. How you respond is a matter of choice. Sometimes it's simpler to regard the conversation as a form of entertainment. The game is all about removing a few (much needed) dollars from your pocket. Whether it be for a mooring or for a fresh mango or for a watchful eye on your dinghy when you go ashore, some sort of transaction can surely be arranged.

Now, it must be said that—like business folk everywhere—the Boat Boys rely on goodwill and the maintenance of their reputation. It's not in their interest to harass, intimidate, or rob their customer base. Word gets around.

But some sailors would prefer to not have to deal with them. Some sailors just don't like to be bothered. But if you treat the Boat Boys as a resource—the same way they look at you—and ask where to get a taxi or where to find fresh batteries, you might be pleasantly surprised by the response. As citizens of the islands, the Boat Boys do feel proprietary about the place—you, after all, are coming to their home. And they do know everything and everyone.

Boat Boys in Tobago Cays

AND EVERYWHERE YOU'LL find a number of local kids who might come to your boat offering ice and a garbage pickup. It's surprising how pleased you are to see someone who is offering what you need, when you need it—and how much you look forward to their arrival, even at 7am, before school starts!

As everywhere, folks are hustling to make a living. They see boat after boat, each worth a half-million dollars or more, come into their local anchorage and the hope arises that maybe they can be of service. A few bucks for a bag of ice makes a big difference to these purveyors, so we try to spread some joy where we can.

As HONORABLE AS the majority of Boat Boys are, you might encounter a few rogues. The usual time to meet such a one is when about to drop anchor. Suddenly, a fast speedboat will buzz up on you and a cheery voice will call out, "You can't anchor there, Cap. No. Bottom no good. Come with me."

And he might lead you to a rather dubious looking rope tied to a bleach bottle and say, "Here you go, Cap. Nice secure mooring for you. Only $30."

Now on a night without a breath of wind and minimal current, you might be lucky and get away with it. But if the Cruising Guide suggests there's decent holding in the bay, stay with your first plan and politely—or forcefully, if necessary—go with your original decision.

13

Talk Radio

As the world of electronics grows continually more sophisticated, the gear we see on new boats has grown ever more complex and capable. That trusty standby of marine communication, the VHF radio, now sports many new refinements—though not all of these will be activated on the unit aboard your charter bareboat. But the VHF will be a constant part of your daily routine, so make sure that the boat briefer instructs you in detail how it works. They come from various manufacturers and each has its power, volume, and squelch controls in different places—so familiarity with one brand may not be helpful when faced with a new one. And be sure to do a radio check before you leave the base.

Have a couple of crew sit in on the VHF briefing—they can pass on the knowledge to the others. It is an essential piece of safety equipment and may be a literal life saver. In addition, it will be in use several times each day for making dock or dinner reservations, hailing dive boats, checking weather forecasts, etc.

While we generally advise against relying on your mobile phone for making emergency calls, some Caribbean jurisdictions—the

British Virgin Islands, for one—have emergency services that do not monitor VHF frequencies at all. So if an emergency should arise, use the VHF for an initial call and to monitor responses (with VHF, you may get assistance from a nearby boat, for instance), but also use your phone to call the emergency numbers as provided by the charter company.

Expect to see emergency information posted to the bulkhead at the Nav station.

In the BVI, channel 16 calls are monitored by US Coast Guard personnel from the US Virgin Islands or Puerto Rico, and requests for assistance may be routed to local BVI responders. But a phone call to the all-volunteer BVI Search and Rescue (VISAR) will probably have a quicker response. (On all bareboats, there is generally a notice stuck to the bulkhead by the navigation station with emergency information for the local sailing area. It will be covered in your briefings as well.)

But it's not only the dire emergency that makes the VHF so useful. We've seen inflatable toys fly off the stern of a boat motoring at speed. A quick call on the VHF to 'Power Cat motoring NE off Fat Man Cay' was enough to get them to turn back and grab the wayward flamingo. So, think of the VHF as not only the best way for you to contact the world, but for the world to contact you.

IN GENERAL THOUGH, the VHF is your go-to communications tool. Its defining feature is that it broadcasts to anyone with a working receiver, whereas phones are one-to-one. This broadcasting capability means that aid may be just as likely to come from a nearby vessel or shore-based assistance, as from an official search-and-rescue or emergency responder. Also, rescue services often are able to create a single line of position from just a few seconds of listening to your MAYDAY or other emergency call.

> **NOTE**: *Learn how to change from High to Low power—not to save electricity but to take up less VHF bandwidth. If the marina is one mile away you don't need to broadcast your request (and hog Channel 16) up to 20 miles away.*

ALSO:

- Learn how to adjust the Squelch control, then leave the setting alone during your charter.
- It makes sense to have electronics that are comfortable to use and whose operation is second nature. So, if you own a handheld unit that you are familiar with, bring it along. It can go ashore with the crew and communicate with the mothership, too. Arranging a pickup, for instance. Just don't forget the charger!
- Channel 16 is the universal channel for emergency broadcasts and establishing contact with other vessels or shore-based facilities. It is not a channel for conducting non-essential conversations. Make contact on 16 and switch to 68, 69, 71, or 72. And remember to refer to channel numbers in the form of One-Six, Six-Eight, etc.

Once on Channel 16, you'll hear voice traffic ranging from boats calling marinas, restaurants, and other boats to commercial traffic such as cruise ships or ferries. So Channel 16 is a common, shared resource. Be as brief as possible in establishing contact with the other party before switching to a different channel for the (still brief) conversation. There is a protocol to VHF use that dictates that the party being hailed gets to nominate a channel for both parties to switch to.

LET'S say you are on the vessel Rosebud and are calling the restaurant Rotgut's Rodehouse Your exchange would be something like this:

'Rotgut, Rotgut, Rotgut, this is Rosebud, Rosebud, Rosebud. Over.' The response would be something like:

'Rosebud, this is Rotgut. ACKNOWLEDGE and Switch to Channel 68. Over.'

Your response would be, 'Rotgut, this is Rosebud. Switching Six-Eight. Over.'

And you would change the channel selector to Channel 68 and commence calling again.

'Rotgut, this is Rosebud. Over.'

You would expect to hear, 'Rosebud, this is Rotgut. How can I help you? Over.' And you would make reservations for lunch or make inquiries etc.

When you have concluded your conversation, finish by saying 'Rotgut, thank you. This is Rosebud switching back to Channel 16. Rosebud, out.'

THE OBJECT IS to speak clearly, not quickly. Use the term 'Over' at the end of each segment of the conversation, until you've reached the end. Then say, 'Out' to signal that you are concluding the conversation.

Note the triple use of the restaurant's name and the boat's name, initially at least.

Is it strictly necessary? In general use, you might only say the name twice, but if you were on the high seas and hoping to attract attention you should indeed follow full protocol and use the triple-term call.

Occasions for hailing on VHF:

- When approaching a marina and requesting a slip or to pick up fuel and water.
- Making a restaurant reservation. A word of caution: In some areas where there is known to be serious crime we would suggest not using your real boat name when calling in, since that could alert possible thieves to your movements. Just use a simple name for the reservation. A friend always calls his boat Mango II, whatever its real name might be. When making an emergency call, or requesting assistance, however, always use the proper name!
- Calling another boat whose name you know, or hailing a party ashore that is operating a handheld VHF unit.
- Responding to a call from someone whose name you don't know or didn't hear clearly. Use the formula 'Vessel calling Rosebud, please go ahead.'

When you are traveling in a convoy with friends, or have another boat you wish to stay in contact with, choose a non-assigned channel —09, 68, 69, 71, for example—as a place to conduct conversations. Ask which is the best to use at the base before you leave. You can continuously monitor this channel along with Ch. 16 and any others you wish.

———

SOME AREAS GIVE the weather forecast in French or Spanish only. The forecast may refer to the Beaufort Scale, such as in the French West Indies where you might hear: '*Nor-est, Cinque, Deux Metres,*' (Wind from the North-east, Force 5 or 17-21 knots, Swell—2 meters or 6.4 feet) for example. When communicating with authorities, you will be expected to use the Standard Phonetic Alphabet. Find the Alphabet and much other useful information in our Safety Packet (Download a copy for the boat).

Since boats get named the strangest things, it may be crucial to know how to spell out your boat name using the phonetic alphabet whether you're booking a table at a restaurant or request immediate helicopter evacuation.

DISTRESS PROCEDURE:

There are levels of urgency associated with emergencies. Some situations require immediate response since a life may be at risk from heart attack, loss of blood, or other trauma. But others, while serious, may not require absolutely immediate response.

Take the example of a vessel under power and getting tangled in some loose fishing nets or hitting floating debris—and knocking out the rudder or jamming the propeller. The vessel may not be able to steer, or may have very restricted capability. Help is required but the boat is afloat and all aboard are safe. A third example is where you wish to convey important information related to safety, such as the presence of a number of floating logs or a sudden squall or waterspout of unexpected severity. In the first instance, the Channel 16 call would be a Distress call, or Mayday. In the second, an Urgent call, or Pan-Pan. The third is a Safety call, or Securité (pronounced *Securitay*).

MAYDAY:

Don't use this unless there truly is a life-threatening emergency—it could be an allergic reaction/ anaphylaxis shock from a jellyfish sting, cardiac arrest, or having to abandon a sinking vessel.

A yacht aground on soft sand in calm conditions wouldn't warrant a Mayday. Though it would if the skipper subsequently suffered a heart attack! When requesting a Mayday response, you are asking for aircraft, helicopters, rescue divers—it's an emergency after all.

The person receiving the call will want to know a lot of information. So when going offshore you should have the information available for immediate access by your crew. It's best presented as a printed card and kept taped to the underside of the chart table top, or someplace close by the VHF station.

WE HOPE you never have to make such a call but if you do, follow this procedure:

First, make sure that your VHF is actually turned on and tuned to Channel 16. Select 25 Watts/HI Power, as you want to broadcast far and wide.

Wait for a gap in conversation if other people are talking and at the first opportunity press the transmit/talk button on the side of the handset. Everyone else making routine calls will stop talking after you say the following words. If people keep talking, don't wait for them to pause but begin with BREAK, BREAK, BREAK.

Then say slowly and clearly:

MAYDAY, MAYDAY, MAYDAY, then (without waiting for a response):

- **WHO** you are (vessel's name)
- **WHERE** you are (Your position in Latitude /Longitude from the chart or GPS, or a bearing and distance from a widely known geographical point.)
- **WHAT** is wrong (nature of distress or difficulty).
- **KIND** of assistance desired.
- **NUMBER** of persons aboard and condition of any injured.
- **SEAWORTHINESS** status of your vessel
- **DESCRIPTION** of your vessel—length, type, cabin, mast, power (sail or motor), color of hull, charter company

that you're with, superstructure and trim (listing, foundering etc).

- **RADIO** channel you are monitoring. It's important to make a communications schedule.
- **SURVIVAL EQUIPMENT** available (i.e.. rafts, etc.)

NOTE: *It is important that you give the full range of information since conditions could change and you lose power to your radio. A mariner listening may have a chance to write down the information or it could be received by a Coast Guard unit that records all Channel 16 traffic.*

Release the transmit/talk button and wait for acknowledgment. Keep listening on Channel 16 for instructions. Appoint a crew member to monitor the VHF for response.

If no response is forthcoming, then repeat the distress call.

Of course, if you should hear a MAYDAY call, write down salient details that you could pass on to the appropriate parties. Respond to the MAYDAY call to:

1. Confirm to the caller that someone has heard them, and
2. Gather information that you might be able to pass on by calling the Coast Guard on Ch. 16.

   NOTE: *The original caller's signal might be able to reach you but not strong enough to be picked up 50 miles away by Coast Guard antennas.*

RADIO CHECK

The radio check is an important part of familiarization with your equipment. It is not a test you need to make every day. Do it once on the dock with the base operator.

The first test is simply to ascertain that the unit is functional. On the dock you'll probably hear back from the dockmaster who might be a few boat lengths away.

The usual procedure is this:

- Set your unit to Low (power), adjust the Squelch setting and go to Channel 16 where you say:
- 'Any station, any station. This is Mango, Mango, looking for a radio check. Over.'
- Ideally you will get a response like this:
- 'Vessel calling for a radio check, this is Tuna, Tuna Receiving you loud and clear from Turtle Cay.'

'Loud and Clear' may also be expressed as paired numbers from 1 to 5 as in, '3X5' (moderate volume/maximum clarity) though '4X5' or '5X5' are the general responses. 'Turtle Cay' is wherever the responding vessel is located. Now you have a good idea of the state of the call and the distance it can be heard. You may get several responses. All the better.

NOTE: *we say Ch. 16 for the radio check. In areas other than the Caribbean we might suggest 68 or 72 but in the islands there isn't a lot of traffic on those channels so you might not get any responses. Ch. 16 is a good option in this instance. Of course, if there is traffic on Ch. 16, use 68 or 72 etc.*

14

Cat Power

MULTI TASKING

A yacht is an expensive asset to own. Anyone who lives near a marina will have noticed that boats seem to sit in their slips for much of the year—going nowhere and doing nothing. Over recent years, however, the yacht charter business has increased exponentially. Why own a yacht when you can rent one for a week or two in different parts of the world? Or, why not own a yacht in one part of the world that allows you to sail a similar model in different parts of the world whilst yours is earning an income? These aspects of the charter industry are driving its rapid growth and constant innovation.

This change in boating habits has been one of the drivers behind the rapid innovations in yacht construction and design. It is also one reason for the sudden increase in market share for the catamaran sector.

WHAT DESIGN IS BETTER SUITED to a short cruising schedule than the modern catamaran? New materials and design parameters are driving the design of the modern cat with developments like a full en suite bathroom attached to every cabin—an unthinkable waste of space in a traditional cruising monohull. The innovations in materials—making for a lighter, stronger construction—along with the growth in efficient, short-course sailing instruction have paved the way for a vibrant charter industry, with most of the growth being in the catamaran segment.

Many of the new catamaran sailors have crossed over from monohulls, finding the family-friendly space and level sailing to be sufficient inducements. These sailors are seeing the wisdom in the rallying cry:

'Once you go Cat, you never go back!'

———

THE TRANSITION from monohull to catamaran, or from single-engine to twin, can be complicated if the subtleties of catamaran operation—particularly when under power—aren't fully understood. And it is under power that the sailor will spend their first hour or so while getting underway from the dock and preparing the sails for hoisting.

WE SUGGEST the new crew actually spend a little time practicing maneuvers in and around the departure point.

- Start with slow approaches to a buoy or marker employing crew hand signals and operator's throttle control.
- If you have electronic throttles, notice the slight delay between your hands' input and the propellers' output. More on this later.
- Spin the boat 360 degrees by opposing engine thrust alone.
- Observe the action of the wind on the vessel—notice how it speeds you up (when from behind). Slows you down (when from ahead). Pushes you sideways (when on the beam). And a combination thereof (when coming at an angle).

- Activate the autopilot. See how it responds to inputs.
- Run a slalom course down a row of empty mooring balls.
- Do it in reverse.
- Play with the catamaran while you have some time and it is all new.
- Drop the anchor (in a safe area) to see how quickly the windlass will respond.
- Get organized. You don't want to arrive in a crowded mooring field at dusk and try to sort it all out under pressure. We've tried that ourselves and do not recommend it.

OPERATING a catamaran under power is a very precise operation. The widely spaced engines coupled with efficient propellers and a shallow draft mean you have the torque to turn the vessel 360 degrees in its own length. The very same shallow draft coupled with a high superstructure can also mean the vessel is sometimes blown around in strong winds, however. But powerful engines can help.

NOTE: *By applying one, off-center engine in forward gear, your cat will go ahead and rotate away from that force. By powering the other engine in reverse, you can eliminate that forward component and just have the rotation. This is known as a Pivot Turn. When making a pivot turn on a cat with fixed (non-folding/feathering) propellers, you'll get approximately 20% less thrust in reverse than you'd get in forward gear. So, to rotate without going forward, you'll need to give the reverse engine slightly more revs than the forward one.*

IN GENERAL, the longer the catamaran's waterline, the smoother the ride will be. Short waterlines can lead to 'hobby-horsing' in swell or chop. Charter groups often load their cats with plenty of toys, which can cause complications if items such as SUPs (Stand-Up Paddleboards) are not properly attached to railings or deck fittings. A sudden squall can tear those items loose and send them flying— which is true of towels, swimsuits, coffee cups, and all kinds of small items. Keep them tied off or tidied away. And, when underway at perhaps 10 knots, the resulting airflow on deck will be at least that, and probably more depending on the prevailing wind, so the risk is always present. It is a good idea to appoint someone to supervise the 'deck risk' and make sure all loose items are secured.

Now, it is obviously true that every sailboat is a powerboat—at least until the sails go up.

One obvious difference between a catamaran and other motor-driven vessels is that it sits largely *on* the water rather than *in* the water and, because of its widely spaced engines, is highly maneuverable.

And because those engines are only relatively powerful, and the vessel not appreciably heavier for its length than, say, a similarly sized monohull--a typical 45-foot monohull might displace 25,000 lbs and be powered by a 55HP engine, while a common 45-foot cat displaces 32,000 lbs and has twin 45HP engines. Given its small underwater profile and the widely spaced engines, however, the catamaran is generally more responsive to the throttle. Most cats will have an electronic throttle and some a mechanical cable-connected control. In either case, care must be taken when operating these controls, particularly with the electronic throttle, because:

- There is a slight delay between movement of the controls and response from the engine, causing the boat to possibly surge ahead if too much power is applied in the mistaken belief that the throttle isn't responding. This may result in discomfort and possible injury to an unwary crew member or guest. And

- because the throttle controls lack the friction inherent in cable-led controls and so offer no resistance to inputs—making it likely the operator might apply too much grunt inadvertently.

ONE WAY of handling the electronic throttle is to wrap a finger and thumb around the base of the electronic control lever—almost like holding a pen or pencil—and bracing with the three other extended fingers against the console or throttle housing.

This allows for quite firm control over the movement of the throttle by rolling the wrist forward and back. Very small movements of the throttle will result in sharp increases of power at the propeller. As there are two throttles, two hands need to be working at the same time—unlike, say, a displacement vessel, where a heavy hand on the throttle will be counterbalanced by the large weight of the boat—which will be slow to respond. And in a similar fashion, the light weight of the catamaran and its small wetted surface area will allow it to continue gliding after power is reduced.

But a short burst on the engines will slow it right down. So you have to be careful with the throttles in order to avoid a herky-jerky response. If the yacht has mechanical cable-connected throttle controls, more pressure is often needed and the controls may be handled with a firm grip atop the throttle.

HAVING SEEN how slick and swift the cat can be, it will be time to go sailing. First, let's look at the basic characteristics of the modern cruising catamaran:

Anyone who has even a modest interest in sailing craft will be aware of the incredible innovations made by catamaran designers for such high-profile ventures as the several offshore round-the-world racing competitions. Massive sail area, wings, foils—while most of these innovations may not trickle all the way down to the modest charter cats, the principles still apply. Large sail area means extra power. Light weight means that power is more usable.

ASPECTS of the catamaran to consider—let's call them *catributes* —are:

- The lack of a backstay. Allowing for
- A very large roach—additional sailcloth—in the freed-up area at the after end of the mainsail.
- Newer sail designs that incorporate that extra fabric all the way to the top of the mast in the Square-top style.
- Aerodynamic theory will define that extra roach as the source of increased power.
- In order to absorb that power, the fabric must be heavier.
- Accordingly, lengthy fiberglass or carbon fiber battens are inserted the full width of the sail.

NOTE: *The benefits and attributes listed above will not be applicable to any catamaran which has an in-mast furling main.*

ALSO:

- The lack of backstay requires that shrouds be brought much further aft than on a monohull, limiting how far out you can ease the mainsail downwind.
- The forward-facing strut sometimes added halfway up the front of the mast to keep it 'in column' can chafe on the jib during tacking and heave-to maneuvers.

And, because catamarans don't heel to any appreciable degree, they fully utilize that power as compared with monohulls, which lose a lot of power by spilling the wind off and over the top of the sail as they heel. This is of course a safety feature on the monohull—in that the rig doesn't get overpowered, since more power creates more on-board loads. That's why the size of the catamaran's mast itself, along with the gauge of the wire shrouds and the weight of the mainsail's cloth will likely be twice that of a same-length monohull. Of course all this heavy mainsail weight (extra roach and long battens) has to be raised before it can be useful.

Consequently, the simple halyard familiar to the monohull sailor won't do the job.

- A compound 2:1 ratio halyard,
- with one end of the halyard secured at the top of the mast,
- is led down to and through the head block on the sail and back up to the top of the mast.
- It then runs down the inside of the mast to exit close above deck level.
- The mechanical purchase this creates makes it easier to raise the heavy sail--but it does lead to a big pile of line once it's fully hoisted AND a lot of line to run back through rope clutches and sheaves when the mainsail is dropped.
- So it's important that crew learn how to figure-eight rather than just coil what will easily be 150' or more of halyard.

When raising the cat's mainsail, crew need to be vigilant in making sure that the sail—and in particular the ends of the battens—won't get caught in the lazyjack lines that support the canvas stack pack. Post a spotter to monitor the situation as you hoist. This is an impor-tant job for someone (an older child, perhaps) who lacks the requi-site physical strength—it'll make them feel useful at a critical part of the day. Simply have the spotter stand somewhere safe and with a good sightline to the sail and say to the person working the halyard:

'*Go, go, go,*' when the sail is clear to do so.

'*Stop, stop, stop,*' before the sail gets caught.

'*Down, down, down,*' if a batten snags a lazy jack and needs to come down a bit to be freed.

All this extra roach means that the sail must be kept to one side of the boom topping lift—preferably the side that the main halyard block is on when compared with the topping lift block at the top of the mast. You want to avoid a tangle at the masthead. So, take a look up top and see which block is to port and which to starboard— and align the sail accordingly. Use the ship's binoculars if necessary.

You'll be pointing head-to-wind while raising the mainsail. Keep plenty of slack in the mainsheet so the sail and boom can swing freely—weather vane—during the constant shifts.

Once the mainsail is up, take a couple of wraps around the main-sheet winch and bear away/fall off to whatever course you're following that day. But keep running your engines (or at least the windward one) in forward gear. Cats don't perform well under mainsail alone. Generally, cruising cats tend to round up under mainsail alone, without the jib to balance the big roachy main. So you may have to counter this weather helm with power from the windward engine. And leave it running until the jib is unfurled and properly trimmed--at which time you can turn the engine off.

Raising the main at anchor

On a catamaran, when raising the main whilst on mooring ball or at anchor, you can use differential (opposite) thrust to keep the cat aligned head to wind instead of letting it naturally yaw to port or starboard of it. (Make sure that you're holding position and not advancing the cat forwards as you do this). This is an especially useful trick on the increasingly popular 'square top' mainsails when, about halfway up the hoist, the time comes to get the sail to the left or (more usually) right of the boom topping lift in order to avoid a crossed line at the sheaves at the masthead.

Without a boom vang—the system used to apply downward pressure to the boom in order to control the shape of the sail—you'll be using either your mainsheet traveler or the so-called German-style twin mainsheet to exert such pressure and so control mainsail twist profile. *Twist* is simply the term used to describe how the back edge of a sail falls away from the wind toward the top. You definitely want some—but you need to know how to control it.

LET'S SPEAK GERMAN:

Many modern catamarans utilize a system known as the German mainsheet--which is unlike the traditional arrangement, where a single line passes through multiple blocks (pulleys) that connect the movable boom to the deck of the boat. In both instances, the mainsheet will be attached where it exerts the most leverage—at the end of the boom. Traditional mainsheets then cascade through blocks down to a traveler track which runs crosswise across the 'back porch' rooftop.

German mainsheet setup with double lines for positioning laterally (windward) and tensioning vertically (leeward).

Usually, the sheet's attachment point is to a car that runs on this traveler track for 15-20 feet (depending on the size of the boat). Using its own control lines which run through its own blocks, the traveler can be adjusted to position the mainsheet to windward or leeward of the centerline—or if you're not sure what to do with it (or shorthanded...or, possibly, feeling a bit lazy) just left in place on the centerline.

Through such means, which effectively creates a movable attachment point for the traveler, vertical (downward) as well as lateral (sideways) pressure can be exerted on the boom to control the degree of twist in the leech of the mainsail.

In the German system the traveler track and its car, blocks, and control lines are dispensed with. Instead, the mainsail trimmer is offered two mainsheets that run from the boom and are led down either side of the boat to winches by the helm station--or sometimes they share a winch. The idea of the German system is that you locate the boom *laterally* with the windward sheet by moving it in or out from the boat's centerline, and position it *vertically* with the leeward sheet—like a more powerful boom vang—to bring the back end of the boom either down (to decrease twist) or easing it up to increase twist.

The advantage of replacing the traditional traveler system on a cruising boat is the elimination of the various control lines and multiple blocks—any one of which can create a tangle which needs to be released by a hapless crew member stretched across the wide rooftop. With a traditional mainsheet arrangement you vang the mainsail using a combination of mainsheet and very wide traveler track—around 15-20'—far longer than on any monohull of the same length. On a cat with the German system, you won't have a traveler. You'll vang the mainsail using the triangulation technique just described.

How to handle these two lines in routine trimming and in maneuvers such as tacks—and especially jibes—is not a technique that's usually gone into in any depth at the dockside boat briefing.

The bareboat skipper is expected to either know and care—or not. If you don't know, don't care, and therefore don't ask, and don't find out—don't worry, you'll be in good company! We often see charter boats with these systems sailing around less efficiently and, as a result, less speedily, but nonetheless oblivious to the consequences. Nothing really bad will likely happen as a result. But you'll have a much easier time of it—and sail faster and more comfortably—if you use the German mainsheet system in the way it was intended. It's really not that hard!

Tacking

When you're tacking, you're heading upwind through a series of zig-zags. On a cruising cat, these won't be the familiar 90-degree right angles but a more typical 100 degree—or in choppy seas, 120 degrees. Whichever mainsheet system you have, you should adjust it to keep the boom close to the centerline. Maybe a little to windward of the centerline in a moderate 15-knot breeze and smooth seas, and a little below it in stronger 20+ knot wind and choppier conditions. Many cruisers ignore the mainsheet entirely in tacks and focus on the jib alone. They leave the boom roughly centered. If they're aware of this at all, they are willing to sacrifice the balance and performance enhancing properties that the fine tune of this powerful sail can offer. They're on vacation after all.

Jibing

This is where things can get hairy and you'd be much safer—and feel more in control—if you go through the right steps, especially in a fresh breeze over 17-21 knots true.

When you're sailing downwind on a cruising cat with a standard issue jib and main, you're going to be sailing at a slightly higher angle to the wind in order to get the jib out of the wind shadow of your boat's big, roachy mainsail—which, itself, can't be eased to far out because of the shrouds being so far aft. So, in order to maintain a healthy VMG, you'll be jibing through a bigger angle: 70-80 degrees.

Whichever mainsail you have, the Number 1 rule is that the helmsman steers the boat *verrry slooooowly* through the jibe in order to allow the crew member(s) time to do what they need to do.

> **NOTE**: *Turning too quickly is the biggest cause of bad and dangerous jibes on cruising boats. Match your rate of turn to the speed at which your crew can do what needs to be done to the main sail.*

With a *TRADITIONAL* mainsheet and traveler the sequence is as follows:

- After the skipper gives the command 'Prepare to jibe' the crew position themselves, prepare their lines and winches and reply 'Ready'.
- At the next command 'Jibing' (meaning that the helmsperson is turning the boat), grind the traveler car from its leeward-most position all the way to the centerline while simultaneously, if you have enough crew, bringing in the single mainsheet.
- The object is to get the main boom centered to avoid a shock-inducing 'slam' of the mainsail/boom after crossing the dead-downwind line.
- f the boat you're on has two separate winches for the traveler and mainsheet and you've got two capable crew, the last two steps can be done simultaneously.
- If traveler lines and mainsheet are led to the same multipurpose winch—or you've only got one reliable

crewmate, break these tasks into two and do them in series rather than parallel.

- First, center and secure the traveler after 'Ready to jibe' and before you reply 'Ready'. Even with electric winches, things can happen quickly during a jibe and 'one person/one job' is the rule.
- Halfway through the jibe, immediately after the boom commits to the new side, both traveler and mainsheet must be eased to their new positions to avoid being over-trimmed:
- Drop the traveler car (under control) all the way to the new leeward and ease the mainsheet out—but not so far that the sail's battens are hard against the spreaders. Again, if winches and capable crew numbers allow, both these jobs can be done simultaneously. If not,
- Drop the traveler, then ease the main. Either way, it's very important to get that big sail to its new position as quickly as possible as it's under a lot of pressure.

WITH *GERMAN-STYLE* TWIN MAINSHEETS, the sequence is as follows:

- After the skipper gives the command 'Prepare to jibe' the crew prepare themselves and when so organized, reply 'Ready'
- At the next command 'Jibing' (meaning that the helmsperson is turning the boat), ease the leeward mainsheet enough to winch the windward mainsheet so as to bring the boom close to the centerline.
- Once roughly centered, lock off the windward sheet, take out any slack from the leeward sheet and prepare it around a winch so that it can be quickly eased under control (for this old leeward sheet is about to become the new windward sheet).
- Immediately after the boom commits to the new side, ease

the new windward mainsheet that you've got ready on a winch. Don't let the sail's full-length battens press against the shrouds or spreaders, though.

- Then, load up the leeward sheet on a winch and grind down the back end of the boom--which, without taking this step, will be a couple of feet higher than it should be for optimal twist.
- Again, if winches and capable crew numbers allow, both these jobs can be done simultaneously. If not, do them in sequence--but quickly. Either way, it's very important to get that big sail to its new position as it's under a lot of pressure.

NOTE: *As we've mentioned previously, whichever mainsheet system you have, the crew will have a much safer and stress-free jibe if the person at the helm takes the boat very slowly through the turn—even stopping the turn temporarily at dead downwind if necessary to allow crew to catch up and be ready for the all-important release.*

APPARENT WIND EFFECT **during the jibe**.

When you're sailing downwind on a cat you're going to be sailing faster than a monohull. The boat's narrow hulls and lack of heavy keel also give it an inherent advantage over monohulls. And the absence of a backstay means that your mainsail will have more roach and be more powerful than on a similarly-sized monohull. Even better, the apparent wind will feel correspondingly lighter than it truly is. So far, so good.

But during the jibe maneuver, as you begin to turn downwind, you'll sheet in your mainsail hard, albeit temporarily. Both these actions will slow you down. But the true wind will still be blowing.

So you, on your temporarily slower boat—and the big sail above you—will feel a seemingly stronger apparent wind than you felt while you were tearing along with speed. This is why it's important to steer a super-slow turn—not just to get the boom centered before the jibe, but to get it eased out immediately after.

> **NOTE**: *Because catamarans don't heel to any appreciable degree as an indicator of power, crew need to pay extra attention to weather helm and rudder angle—and to leeward shroud floppiness—to ensure it's not over-powered. OR: If everyone near me--and going in the same direction as I am-- is reefed, then maybe I should be, too!*

CHECK the ship's electronic rudder indicator to see the amount by which your rudder is off-center in order to keep the boat tracking straight. This is the amount of weather helm you're carrying. A little (4-6 degrees) is actually good but anything above 10 degrees needs to be addressed — it's not only uncomfortable to steer, it's also not fast.

Possible reasons for that 10 degrees (or more) are:

1. You may have a tad too much mainsail up. Or,
2. You have either the mainsheet or traveler trimmed too tight —or too close to the boat's centerline.

To decide which, remember the adage: *when in doubt, ease it out*—the amount that you can ease out a sail before it starts to luff (flutter) at its leading edge is the amount by which that sail was over-trimmed. So first try easing the mainsheet(s) and or traveller (if you have one).

If you still have too much weather helm, even with the front edge of the mainsail luffing, then you've likely got too much mainsail up and it's time to reef it.

(But, if you've still got a big genoa/jib out—one that overlaps the mast—try rolling up about a quarter of it, removing the overlap. That alone might do the trick before you need to reef the mainsail.)

Pinching (pointing too close to the wind) when going upwind has a higher penalty in a cat: speed will be reduced quickly due to lack of momentum-giving ballast keels and you'll go sideways swiftly (because those keels are stubby). Try sailing just a bit lower—especially in choppy seas. This is what is known as sailing 'full and by'.

Cats are trimmed with way more **twist** in their sails than monohulls because they sail faster and so the apparent wind angle changes more quickly the higher up the mast you go.

Furthermore, twist is also a great way to dump power in marginal conditions that don't really need a full reef. Because cats are designed without a boom vang they actually self-twist—unless cranked down tight by mainsheet/traveler tension.

15

Puff Piece
READING THE WIND

S ailing is largely a matter of managing the relationship between the boat and the wind. Sometimes you'll see a boat cruising happily along in a brisk breeze when suddenly it seems to run out of puff—the jib flapping, boat speed dropping. This happens when the wind has shifted forward unexpectedly—*headed*—and the crew haven't seen it coming or responded quickly enough.

Likewise, a boat might suddenly round up wildly into the wind as a gust *lifts*—shifts aft relative to the boat—overwhelming the sail plan and rudders, catching the crew by surprise. These events are caused by a sudden change in the relationship between boat and wind speed and direction.

THE CRUCIAL ELEMENT is the wind—you need to be able to feel it and, even better, 'read' it—in advance of its getting to you, since sometimes if you can feel the change, it's already too late. Better to see it coming and act preemptively. And yes, you can read the wind. All around you the sea surface is covered with signs revealing the wind direction and speed. The clouds above, seaweed strung out in long lines—all tell the story of the wind and its direction. Smooth water reflects light better than rougher water…you get the picture. This texture/shading of the sea surface will give you an indication of the upcoming micro wind speed changes.

FOR MORE CONSISTENT, macro, changes, the trusty Beaufort Scale has precise descriptions of sea states and their related wind speeds. For example, whitecaps will first begin to show at around 10 knots of wind and be really apparent at about 13 knots.

Most people, of course, can roughly tell which way the wind is blowing. From the left, right, in front, behind—good enough for a swing on a golf course, perhaps, but not for sailing a boat. A couple of turns of the head will be enough to orient you. Just compare the wind pressure for left and right ears—you can hear the whooshing sound as it slips past. When you have equalized that sound, you'll be head-to-wind.

When sailing, take time to remove/roll up the helm station's weather curtains—unless it's raining, of course—that way you'll have a much better sense of the wind.

Sometimes a simple splash of water on the cheeks or back of the neck can tell you where the wind is. Or, just lick your finger and hold it high

READING the wind allows you not only to see what the wind is doing at that moment but, by looking farther afield, you can see what the wind will be doing in just a few moments. By reading the puffs on the surface of the water you can see whether you'll be headed (forced to apparently fall off the wind) or lifted (able to apparently point higher), though of course you'll still maintain the same angle to the wind. It's just that the wind has moved around by 5 degrees or more due to a change in wind speed—technically called a 'velocity shift'.

Good race crews hone this skill since it can indicate when it's the right time to tack or jibe. (If you're constantly being headed, and therefore sailing further away from your destination, it's time to tack to take advantage of it--you'll sail closer to your destination on the next leg.)

WHEN SAILING IN THE CARIBBEAN, where many islands have steep hills overlooking the ocean, try at least once to climb the hills a bit and look down on the yachts sailing the channels. Observe the wind direction as indicated by the puffs on the sea surface and see how the boats react as the wind changes direction and speed. You'll easily be able to spot the great sailors from the good ones by the relative boat speeds on similar-sized boats. Not only will you benefit from the hike but you'll get a good sense of just how far away from the islands you'll need to sail to enjoy a consistent breeze.

THE AIR APPARENT

Your boat's wind instruments can read both True and Apparent wind direction but are usually set to a default Apparent Wind mode which means that they are taking into account the boat's speed through the water (or, more correctly, speed through the air) to give you the apparent wind speed and direction.

A typical wind instrument display

Without getting into the vector mathematics of it, what this means is that when you are sailing at 45 degrees to the true wind, your wind instrument will tell you that you are sailing at about 35 degrees.

> **NOTE**: *Don't be tricked into thinking that you're a better sailor than you are, because no bareboat can sail that close to the wind.*

When going upwind, the apparent wind will feel (and read on your instruments) as being stronger than the true wind and when going downwind the apparent wind speed readout will indicate less wind than there truly is.

It's all relative.

16

Cranked Up
FAST + BALANCED

The wind can be fickle and mustn't be wasted—yet most cruising sailors seem to feel that they needn't bother about efficient sailing.

Why go fast?' they seem to be thinking. 'We're cruising!'

But the wind can die down, leaving you with miles to go—miles that you might have already covered had you been sailing fast and efficiently. It's not just a matter of sailing the right way, but of sailing the smart way. The skills involved can be life-saving when you're making a long crossing or dodging an oncoming squall.

AND WHO CARES ABOUT BALANCE? 'We're not walking a tightrope, we're bareboating!'

But a well-balanced boat is one that steers easily. Where the helmsman isn't wrestling with the wheel to keep the boat on track. That smoothness is the result of the balance between the mainsail and the foresail. It's the shape and the size of each of those sails individually that provide the power for the boat—and the same shape and size collectively provide the balance. More power in the jib, let's say, and less in the main—or vice versa—will provide the correct balance for the sea state and the wind speed.

As your sails bend the wind around their area and shape—aspects you control by either reefing (area) or trimming (shape)—they provide your boat with power. You can change the shape and angle of your sails to give you as much, or as little, as you need, depending on what the wind is doing and how fast you want to travel.

Of course, you're still cruising and not racing but there's always the need for speed. You want to get to the anchorage or mooring field to secure the best, safest spot; you want to get to your destination early so that you can enjoy it longer; you want to sail faster than the boat sailing parallel to you, just for the fun of it.

Since you're on a bareboat, you'll be on a catamaran with two sails, not one equipped with a spinnaker or a *Code Zero*. The shape and angle of the two sails you have relative to each other will affect how easy and comfortable the boat will be to drive.

ALL SAILBOATS HAVE a pivot point close to the middle of their hulls around which they turn one way or another. A boat is balanced when its tendency to pivot toward the wind is exactly counterbalanced by its tendency to pivot away from the wind.

Simply put, the sail mostly behind the pivot point (the mainsail) makes the boat turn toward the wind while the sail mostly in front of the pivot point (the jib or genoa) makes the boat turn away from the wind.

A catamaran, of course, has two hulls. The pivot point actually moves around the vessel between the two hulls and is placed a little on the leeward side of the boat—more so when beating upwind in a stiff breeze.

NOTE: *The tendency to turn toward the wind is* weather helm. *The tendency to turn away from the wind is* lee helm.

When we're sailing across or away from the wind, the goal would be to balance the sails so that there is neither weather nor lee helm. But when we're sailing against the wind's general direction (sailing to windward—especially sailing close-hauled) that's not what we want to achieve. This is because sailboats go faster upwind with a small amount of weather helm. How small? About 4-6 degrees of helm. You can measure this using your boat's rudder angle indicator (it's part of your autopilot display even without the pilot being engaged).

Sailing close-hauled is when you most often feel excessive (10 degrees, or more) weather helm. This, along with heeling, is one of the earliest indications that your boat is overpowered, meaning that the sails are generating more power than you can manage. Rudder angles of 10 or more degrees to the centerline are no longer providing beneficial lift, but detrimental drag. It's also very hard on the helmsman's arms and will cause the boat to round up into the wind—especially during gusts. Worse, you'll also be sliding sideways due to excessive leeway.

VELOCITY MADE GOOD: The technical skills needed to effectively sail a boat upwind and down—maximizing sail trim, steering accurately, are all well and good. But they don't mean much if you aren't able to get the boat moving towards your ultimate destination. The key to understanding how well you are doing in this regard is the datum known as VMG, or *Velocity Made Good.*

THE *VELOCITY* PART is easy to understand: it just means speed.

The *Made Good* part is also pretty easy to understand. It is simply a way of expressing how rapidly you are approaching your destination rather than merely the speed at which you're going through the water or, more correctly, over the ground below (SOG), since there may be current adding to or subtracting from the wind-generated pace of the boat.

The basic concept turns on the fact that sailing closest to the wind is not necessarily the fastest point of sail. So if going upwind, it may be advantageous to sail a lower-but-faster course on each tack.

How much lower and how much faster varies with the conditions of the day, the type of vessel being sailed and other factors.

The instruments on your boat will be sufficient to give you the data —Course Over Ground (COG) and Speed over Ground (SOG)— you require to make decisions about the course you need to sail. And if you add a GPS waypoint at your destination and then change your chart plotter's screen to the different views available (scroll through to it by pressing the Page button) you'll get an actual real-time output of your VMG as well as SOG and COG.

Though, in simple terms, if you keep the boat in the groove upwind (footing-off a bit in choppy seas) and sail as low as you can go downwind without collapsing the jib, you will achieve optimal VMG—with no need for the magic box.

- *Upwind.* Keep the boat high as possible 'in the groove'—but foot-off a bit, with slightly eased sheets in choppy seas in order to have the power to slice through them.
- *Downwind.* Sail as low as you can go being careful to not collapse the jib. This way you won't be in danger of an accidental jibe.

So to sum up, when sailing, you're going to be in one of two modes—

COURSE MODE:

In this mode, you sail to a course reference which could be a distant island, a landmark on that island or—if you can't see where you're headed—a compass course that you've plotted from a chart or are getting straight from the ship's electronic plotter. When sailing at night—and the skies are clear—you could take your course from the proverbial 'star to steer her by'.

Whatever method, in this mode you're able to follow your course without the need for tacking or jibing—known as fetching your mark i.e. destination. The helm's job is to keep the boat tracking on its desired course while the trimmers' job is to adjust the main and jib to keep the both windward and leeward tell-tales streaming properly by reacting easing or trimming their sheets in response to changes in the apparent wind.

Or,

WIND MODE:

This mode applies when you can't fetch your destination without tacking (if the destination is upwind of you) or jibing (if the destination is downwind). Here, the trimmers' job is to get their sails dialed-in to the required upwind or downwind mode and it is the helm's job to keep the telltales streaming (when going upwind) or on the back edge of the jib collapsing (when going down).

SIMPLER TERMS RELATING to the wind are Higher and Lower —where,

- Higher means closer to the direction the wind is coming from, and
- Lower means further away from where the wind is coming from.

UPWIND

When sailing close-hauled upwind at about 50 degrees to the wind's direction, there is a narrow band in which the sail trim and boat's direction can be perfectly matched.

- Sail *a couple of degrees higher* and the windward telltale will flutter up, down, or around-and-around while the leeward telltale continues to stream straight back.
- Sail *any higher than that* and the whole front edge of the jib will commence shivering (*luffing*) along its entire height.
- Sail *lower by a couple of degrees* and the leeward telltale does the same while the windward telltale continues to stream straight back.
- Sail *any lower than this* and both telltales will collapse and the wind will appear to have 'apparently' died—check your windex at the top of the mast (or your instruments if you must) and you'll see that you're probably at right angles to the wind and not 45 degrees.

This magical *zen-like* state when sailing upwind, where both leeward and windward telltales are streaming straight backwards, is known as being 'In the Groove'.

ONE WAY TO remember the proper way to manage this is by keeping in mind the phrase, 'Step away from the edge!'

It's a reminder to sail as close to the midpoint of the narrow band as possible.

Avoiding the edge will help you avoid pinching, which is the term for accidentally—not deliberately—steering too close to the wind when sailing close-hauled.

Deliberately but temporarily steering a tad (1-5 degrees) higher when sailing close-hauled is called feathering—which is a proper way to correctly handle wind gusts. A gust (or its opposite, a lull) will also manifest itself as a shift in the direction of the apparent wind— a velocity shift—and by steering higher (or lower, in a lull) you're actually just maintaining your optimal VMG angle to the true wind.

The groove, as the term implies, is pretty narrow. Staying in it is the goal when sailing close-hauled, as you're then converting the maximum possible wind energy into forward rather than sideways heel or backwards drag.

> **NOTE**: *if your high (windward) side telltale flutters, you're too high. If low (leeward), you're too low!*

> *Sail too high and you'll be pinching. All at once you'll notice: The boat will slow down dramatically. You'll make more leeway (slip further sideways to leeward).*

> *The steering wheel will lose feel—it'll seem less heavy (resistant) as you'll have to use much less force to counteract the boat's tendency to steer you toward the wind (weather helm).*

> *Sail too low and your 'V' speed through the water goes up (you sail quicker) but your VMG goes down (you sail further).*

So, when close-hauled, steer to your jib telltales and

- if the windward one is fluttering, steer lower;
- if the leeward one's fluttering, steer higher.
- In a moderate breeze, drop the boom about 6-12 inches (using traveler or mainsheets) at a time as the breeze increases to keep the weather helm, as experienced at the wheel, below 10 degrees reading off the autopilot rudder indicator.
- At all times, trim your mainsheet so that the sail's top-batten telltales stream half of any given time period (10 seconds, say) but are sucked behind the sail on its leeward side the other half.

TACKING

An increasing proportion of new catamarans sacrifice some perfor-mance in order to have self-tacking jibs. If this isn't your choice, when tacking, maintain power in the jib as long as possible (without backing the sail) before releasing the old and trimming the new working jib sheets—and be sure to effect the release before coming head to wind. Whichever jib you have, the modern cruising catamaran tacks through about 100 degrees and will lose forward momentum quickly during the tack and until the sails fill on the new tack. So don't turn the rudders too quickly as that will slow you down as the large flat surfaces of the rudders turn face-on to the water rushing underneath the boat. But don't turn as slowly as in a jibe as, unlike that maneuver you are unpowered during a tack. Rather, make a smooth and steady turn.

DOWNWIND

When the destination is directly downwind of you there is an optimum point of sail analogous to the groove, but not called that. In this situation, it's often more efficient—and a lot safer—to get there by jibing from one deep broad reach to another: the exact angle will vary but you'll be jibing through an angle of around 60 degrees from one tack to another. Achieving this sweet spot when on either tack maximizes your VMG downwind just as keeping in the groove does while going upwind.

So, when on a broad reach: ease both sails out (with the main just lightly touching the spreaders and/or the shrouds) and have the helm steer as low as they can go without collapsing the jib. Sail any lower than this and the entire jib will collapse as the wind will appear to have completely died—check your wind indicator at the top of the mast (or your instruments if you must) and you'll see that you're probably at 180 degrees to the wind and not 30-35 degrees. Steer further the 'wrong' way and you'll find yourself 'sailing by the lee' with the mainsail and its boom on the windward side of the boat instead of the leeward side—not good.

Just keep the jib on the edge of collapsing—but not completely collapsed—and you'll be fine and in no danger of an accidental jibe. If the helming gets tedious—or the helm needs a break, make sure to put the autopilot into 'wind' mode at around 130/135 degrees port or starboard to the wind. *Do not put the boat on autopilot in course-mode downwind* as a wind shift could easily cause an accidental jibe and they're no fun at all.

THE CATAMARAN's mast-supporting shrouds are led further aft than the corresponding shrouds on a monohull, so you can't ease the main quite as much. You'll sail slightly higher in the catamaran.

Don't forget to move the jib's fairlead cars all the way forward to reduce twist in that sail.

NOTE: *When Reaching (Close Reach, Beam Reach, or anywhere in between) —Sail in course mode. Helm steers to the course; trimmers adjust sails to the wind.*

JIB CONTROL DOWNWIND:

On some modern boats, and on all of the ones with self-tacking jibs, it's impossible to move the jib fairlead far enough forward as you fall off deeper away from the wind—on a broad reach point of sail, for example. The reason it's impossible on self-tackers is that there is no fore-and-aft track to facilitate a move in those directions! On others, the track is often just not long enough.

So how to move the sheet lead forward to reduce the 'twist' in the upper third of the jib's leech where it is spilling away desirable power?

The answer is to use a line arranged to pull the jib's clew where you want it—in this case, forward and down.

The original sheet stays in place so that the new line—called the *Barber hauler*—works with it to 'triangulate' the position of the clew. (The name comes from the sailors who first thought of it: the Barber brothers).

Line set up for Barber Hauler

YOU COULD USE any line that you can find, a spare sheet or even a dock line. If you prefer, and are on a boat with the traditional two sheets, you could even re-lead the 'lazy' windward one to a more forward strongpoint such as a cleat or padeye as in adjusting the jib fairlead.

If your boat has a self-tacking jib, you'll need to add an additional line from the clew of the jib forward as mentioned.

JIBING

When jibing, first center the traveler—if there is one. Then grind-in the mainsheet to get the boom roughly centered. (If you don't have a traveler, you may need to haul in on the windward mainsheet while easing the leeward one).

Meanwhile, the crew at the wheel steers *verrrry slooowly* to give the mainsheet handler time to grind in the main and then remove the handle from the winch so as to ease out the mainsheet following the jibe.

ONCE THE MAINSAIL has settled to its new side, quickly but smoothly ease the mainsheet to position the sail the same distance out as it was before the jibe. Once that's done, ease the traveler down its track and check to make sure that the mainsail is not pressed hard against the leeward spreaders or shrouds. Then it's time to un-back the jib. If you have enough skilled crew, do the jib at the same time as you're jibing. But—unlike a tack—wait for the jib to have definitely crossed to the new side before releasing the old sheet.

17

Gust Management
DEALING WITH UNRULY GUSTS

The wind is not a constant force and doesn't blow steadily as if driven by a giant fan—not often, anyway. It fluctuates, sometimes quite dramatically. Many components contribute to these fluctuations—the topography of the land the wind is flowing over, the temperature of the land or the sea over which it passes. Heat rising from an exposed sandbar or small island can bend the flow of the wind or change its speed.

Sometimes the changes in the wind's force are enough to knock the boat around, and sometimes they are barely noticeable. The good news is you can often continue sailing through a periodic gust—a short blast of wind—without resorting to reefing or adjusting the sail plan in any way.

NOTE: *As the speed of the wind doubles, the force increases by a factor of four.*

Here are two simple techniques that you can use when sailing closehauled or on a broad reach in gusty conditions. Neither requires you do anything to the sails. They work because during a gust, the apparent wind changes direction a little, as well as changing velocity.

CLOSE-HAULED:

The technique of *feathering* means steering a little toward the wind when sailing close-hauled, taking the pressure out of the sails by making the angle of attack less efficient. The increased weather helm you feel at the wheel, caused by the gust, will want to make the boat steer that way automatically, so let it—but in a controlled way, so as not to allow the boat to get so close to the wind that you are in danger of tacking. And don't hold it there for long, either, as you may lose too much speed and stall—that is, lose your ability to steer. Most likely you won't need to, because the gust will have passed by quickly.

REACHING:

The Broad Reach requires actions that are the opposite of those used when handling gusts in an Upwind setting. Here, you steer a little farther away from the wind. You're not Bearing Away, as you're not actually changing your angle to the wind and easing sheets. The leading player, the wind, has undergone a velocity shift (an increase or decrease in wind speed creating a shift in the direction of the *apparent wind*) and you must follow it. Be careful not to go so far as to jibe (or even collapse the headsail completely). As the gust subsides, your collapsing jib will indicate that you need to steer back toward the wind to maintain the broad reach.

When on a close reach (around 60 degrees to the wind) or beam reach (at or around 90 degrees) your best gust management technique is to maintain the present course. Take the pressure off both sails by easing them out for as long as the gust lasts. If you're short handed, spill some pressure off the mainsail by easing down the traveler (if you have one) or mainsheet (if you don't).

If you're fully crewed, ease both jib and main—but just as with feathering, the gust will likely have passed by the time you get around to the headsail. This is one of the reasons why you should always have the clutch of the mainsheet open—to allow for short and sudden dumping (briefly letting the sheet run free) from the mainsheet winch. After the gust passes, bring the traveler or mainsheet back in. If you find yourself having to constantly drop the traveler, then leave it down. And if you're still experiencing too much weather helm after that, it's time to reef.

Using these techniques, you'll find that the boat will become easier to control due to reduction in both weather helm and apparent wind. Plus, you'll be sailing faster and/or closer to your destination for as long as the gust lasts.

REEFING:

As we've discussed, sailing is all about managing the relationship between your boat and the wind. In a charter context, most boats are equipped with a set of general purpose sails, designed for winds within specific ranges—say up to 35 knots of true wind. The ability of the boat to sail safely in the higher ranges—above 25 knots—is conditional upon the sailors' abilities to control the size of the sails themselves.

OPERATING with too much sail in too much wind is asking for trouble. Not only can it become exhausting, but the control of the boat may be snatched from the hands of the sailor as the sail plan is overwhelmed. The catamaran may round up and stall head-to-wind, both hulls trapped in the No-Go zone. Many Sunday Sailors don't get the opportunity to practice their reefing skills—if there's too much wind, they won't leave the dock or they'll drop sail and motor. But when sailing in semi-open water those options aren't always the most practical.

NOTE: *The primary rule of sailing in windy conditions is to **Reef Early and Reef Often**: that is, to reef before the situation demands it.*

SOMETIMES YOU'LL BE out on a breezy day and notice that over time the apparent-wind speed seems to be increasing. It was 20 knots, then 23 and it seems to be heading for 25. The steering wheel is jammed hard to leeward, trying to pull the bow down. You're wondering whether you should reef.

First, what do you have to lose? You might spend a few minutes putting in the reef. Then you'll sail more smoothly and in less anxiety. Your crew will feel happier and you'll probably sail faster as the now more-upright mast and keel work together more efficiently. So then the wind drops down to 15 knots. Did you waste those few minutes? No, of course not—you can proceed happily along with reduced sail for a while.

See what happens. The wind may pick up or it may die altogether.

NOTE: *If you ever ask yourself the question, 'Should I reef?' the answer is always 'Yes.' It's much easier to shake out a reef you no longer need than to set a reef you needed five minutes ago. By simply asking yourself the question, you've also answered it.*

REEFING THE MAIN:

On the charter yacht you'll have roller reefing and furling for your headsail (jib or genoa) and mostly a classic up-and-down mainsail, attached to slugs that slide vertically along a track.

Mainsails come in a variety of reefing configurations, each more complicated than the next. The more complicated varieties are considered to be more convenient—by the salespeople, possibly.

. . .

HERE ARE THE VARIETIES:

Classic Main. You're going to have one of three variations on the slab or jiffy reef system for your main:

1. Single-line
2. Two-line
3. Traditional

All of these mainsail systems are simple, proven reliable, and are used on both bareboats and the latest high-tech world-girdling racing yachts.

They all involve taking in a slab of sail by lowering the sail toward the boom. To do this,

1. Ease the main halyard
2. Set the new tack
3. Stretch out the foot of the newly reduced sail
4. Re-tension the halyard
5. Tension the mainsheet as you resume your point of sail

This is achieved by a pre-set reefing line running through a cringle (grommet) in the luff (front edge) and leech (back edge) of the sail, corresponding to the reef of choice. You will likely have two options: first reef and second (deeper) reef. Each reefing line should be a different color for easy identification.

SOME BOATS MAY HAVE a third reef—used mostly when offshore sailing, where you might encounter prolonged heavy winds. You'll see cringles for this but often no line, since it is unlikely to be needed when on charter. (If the winds were blowing that strongly, you'd have dropped all sail and be proceeding under motor—not an option when many miles out to sea.)

• • •

THE DIFFERENCE between them is simply that:

- the single-line system uses just one pre-rigged line to do the entire job while bringing down both new corners, while the
- two-line system uses separate tack and clew lines and the
- traditional uses just one reef line for the clew—requiring you to go to the mast to pull down and secure the new tack by way of a snap shackle and a strong tape-like strap, or by placing the cringle over a hook.

WHY WOULDN'T everyone choose the single-line system?

One reason is that it requires lots of line—up, down, and along the boom—and, if set up properly, special blocks sewn into the sail to reduce the friction such a system entails.

All of this adds cost and weight, which leads us to the two-line system. This also enables a reef to be taken in from the safety and security of the cockpit but uses much less line and doesn't necessarily require those expensive sewn-in blocks.

So WHY WOULD anyone want to use the traditional system?

Simplicity: Less line to deal with—meaning less friction and its associated menace, chafe. In fact the only downside is that it does require some intrepid soul to go forward to the base of the mast and manually secure the new tack to a pre-rigged fastener (often a snap shackle or a Spectra strop attached to the mast).

PUTTING IN THE REEF:

You can either stop the vessel by heaving-to while making your adjustments with some degree of comfort and leisure, or carry on and adjust the settings whilst underway at speed.

- **Heaving-to**: While we have a chapter devoted to this topic later in the book, we'll just mention it here in the context of reefing. This procedure has the benefit of turning the vessel away from the wind somewhat and reducing spray and other uncomfortable effects.

- Make sure that you heave-to on a tack (port or starboard) that will give you enough sea room. You'll still be technically underway and will carry with you the rights and responsibilities of the tack you choose to be on while hove-to. So, generally,
- starboard tack is preferable over port. You'll be crabbing forwards and sideways during the procedure. When you have tacked the vessel with the jib backed, you'll need to ease the mainsail far enough so there is minimal wind pressure on the sail--and bear in mind that, *if you have a self-tacking jib, you'll need to manually set a stopper in the track--before commencing the maneuver*--in order to back the jib effectively. Or you can:
- **Reef while sailing**: Sail on a Close Reach point of sail (around 60 degrees True). This will not relieve the motion of the boat much, but will keep you off a lee shore if you happen to be dangerously close to one when you decide to reef.

Here's How:

Ease your mainsheet to take pressure off the sailcloth.

- Whichever reef point (first or second) you've tucked in, you'll need to crank back up on the main halyard to establish tension on the luff of the sail.
- Then apply mainsheet tension—but not too much—as most reefs are designed to allow the end of the main boom to be carried higher, out of the way of the larger seas that accompany higher winds.
- If you've chosen the first reef, the second reef line (and the third if you have it) will now be very slack, so pull them in by hand and tidy them up to avoid their

hooking around some fitting or obstruction during a
tack.

- If the conditions allow, and once you're happy with the line
settings, mark the reef line and halyard with a Sharpie and
a piece of masking tape so that you can easily replicate the
setting the next time.

NOTE: *Most of the European-built cats come with black main halyards, so
bring a gold or silver Sharpie for marking purposes.*

And if you have time before starting your charter, and the wind
direction is appropriate, get the crew to practice reefing—and mark
the halyard—while still on the dock.

REEFING AN OVERSIZED GENOA:

Self-tacking catamarans have a jib that occupies just the fore-triangle. But, bareboats generally have a foresail larger than strictly
necessary for upwind work. This extra sail area is very useful when
sailing downwind and in light airs when going upwind.

If this is the case on your boat, your first step at reducing sail should
be to roll up some of that sail (10-15%) before you resort to
reducing the mainsail. It's quicker and easier than adjusting the
main. This 10-15% of the genoa—the part that overlaps the main
(i.e. the mast) is a big contributor to your excessive weather helm.
Take that out of play first. It may be all you need to do.

REEFING THE HEADSAIL:

First make sure you have ample sea room. Commence by easing
both the headsail and mainsail and steer yourself on to a broad-
reach point of sail. You'll be sailing fast, so give yourself plenty of

sea room. As soon as you fall off, you'll feel the apparent wind drop considerably.

Be careful though—you don't want to do an accidental jibe! This won't happen as long as you're careful not to steer yourself past dead downwind (180 degrees). But you need to get pretty close (about 150-160 degrees) to that dead-downwind heading for the jib to collapse. This collapse is very obvious—the headsail appears to deflate and fold into the wind shadow of your mainsail.

Once the headsail has collapsed, don't fall off your course anymore (hand steer by keeping an eye on a landmark, a distant cloud—or your compass, if there is nothing to see ahead for reference).

Or simply press *Auto* on your autopilot in Wind mode—though beware, as the autopilot can wander a lot if the unit's responsiveness isn't set just right. The point is that you don't want to jibe accidentally.

Once the sail has lost its power, ease both sheets whilst maintaining control—though don't ease too much at once or the sail could wrap itself around the forestay. At the same time, pull by hand on the furling line until you've taken in the amount you want. Most foresails have short vertical stripes or a series of dots along the foot of the sail marking the reef points, so use those to guide you.

This is the same procedure as when fully furling the foresail, only now you are taking just a little power out of the sail. To complete the task, move your jib fairleads forward along their tracks commensurate with how much you reefed your jib.

TAKING THE LOAD OFF:

If the working headsail-sheet fairlead car needs to be moved forward or back, it may be too hard to do while it's under load from the sheet.

Here's how to temporarily take the load off the sheet in order to move it:

- Fall off onto a deep broad reach to temporarily collapse the headsail, as you would do when furling it.
- Beware of jibing your mainsail. 140-160 degrees off the wind should be enough to blanket the jib in the wind shadow of the mainsail.
- Keep a steady hand on the helm or activate the autopilot — preferably in 'wind mode'.
- Free-up and take the 'lazy' (non-working) headsail sheet and lead it to the leeward midships cleat.
- Then, temporarily tie it off fairly tight using a cleat hitch.
- Ease the working jib sheet so the load is taken up by the former lazy sheet.
- Move the relevant fairlead.
- Apply the load to the correct working sheet,
- Releasing the sheet you'd tied to the midships cleat.
- Re-lead that sheet to its 'lazy' position, and put back the stopper knot if you'd had to previously untie it.

SHAKING OUT THE REEF:

Once you've decided the reefs are no longer required—the wind has dropped and is expected to stay that way, for example—you'll want to shake out the reef. This is much easier than putting the reef in.

FORESAIL:

Take a couple of turns around a winch with the genoa furling line.

- Attach the genoa sheet to another winch.
- Arrange things—by tacking or jibing, if need be—so you're trimming the genoa sheet on the opposite side of the boat

from the furling line. That way you can use both sheet winches at the same time. If this is not possible because of lack of sea room or other issue, just

- Take the furling line back around one horn of a cleat, or around a helm-seat support, handhold, or anything that's conveniently situated, smooth, and strong. Many charter catamarans have all the sail controls in one central location —often an elevated helm position—making communication and execution relatively easy.

THE IDEA IS TWOFOLD:

1. To control the rate at which the furling line builds up around its drum at the bow without crew getting rope burns on their hands from the friction of a too-fast unfurling. And,
2. To avoid the furling line getting bunched up in a tangle as it enters the rotating drum. Release its clutch and begin to pull by hand, then

- While keeping light pressure on the furling line,
- Crank in the genoa sheet.
- Trim the genoa as desired.
- Take out any remaining slack in the furling line.
- Clutch-down and coil up the remaining furling line, leaving it cow-hitched on the nearby lifeline or wherever it's led back to.

MAINSAIL:

Get on a close-haul to close-reach point of sail— around 60-70 degrees to the wind.

- Ease the traveler first (if you have one) and then your mainsheet(s) until the mainsail is depowered
- Release all the reefing lines.
- Start cranking up the halyard.
- Sail a little closer to the wind to reduce pressure on the sail, grinding in the headsail to avoid its luffing. You can choose to overtrim the headsail so as to backwind the main and further depower it while it's going up.
- Crank the halyard tight and have the grinder, or other observer, keep checking that the sail is not getting snagged. And make sure to keep the reefing line slacked free. Once you're happy with the mainsail halyard tension, re-tension the mainsheet, and take any slack out of the reefing lines.

BROACHING ON A REACH:

When sailing rapidly on a broad reach, there is a risk of broach induced by a rapid acceleration whilst surfing down a big wave on a downwind run. Often, in breezy conditions with a boisterous following sea, the wave will pick up the boat by the stern and send it hurtling down towards the trough in front.

Keeping your course, and not permitting the forces working their dark spells on the boat to dominate, requires preemptive or anticipatory steering. The wave is traveling a mite faster than the boat so its speed gets added to the overall apparent wind, causing heeling and creating weather helm as the balance of mainsail/foresail/hull shape gets distorted.

The helmsman has to react quickly to turn the vessel a little away from the wind, reducing the apparent wind back to manageable levels.

HERE'S HOW:

It's not unlike driving a car at a constant speed while going up and down hills:

As you approach the hill, you'll begin to accelerate just as the car's front wheels reach the upslope of the hill. If you don't, you know that you'll slow down below your target speed. As you reach the top of the hill, you'll take your foot off the gas otherwise you'll go above your target speed.

As the wave approaches, its speed will contribute to the forces acting to make the boat round up. Avoid this by steering away from the wind just as the wave reaches the stern. If you don't, the boat will accelerate and pivot above your target course.

When you feel the wave passing under the boat, reduce your counter-steering pressure on the helm—which will be quite considerable—otherwise you'll steer below your target course and, once again, be in danger of jibing.

18

Wet Work
HEAVY WEATHER

When we talk about heavy weather in the Caribbean we're talking about one of two things:

- Strong to Gale or even Storm force winds resulting from a major meteorological low- (or high) pressure system. This is a macro-scale event that'll be well forecast. Or,
- A Squall. These are comparatively micro-scale weather events that will not be forecast any more than the routine Caribbean forecast of isolated showers.

WHEN CHARTERING, you're not likely to be caught in a hurricane—or even a named storm. These are tracked for days and are well forecast. Your charter company will have called you back to base or directed you to a safe haven before one reaches you.

Squalls are much less easy to predict and much more common. You are bound to see one in the distance, if not get caught up by one. They can be isolated to a small area covering just a few square miles and lasting just five, ten or fifteen minutes, though it might feel like longer!

If you're observant, you can often tack or jibe away from an approaching isolated squall and dodge it completely. Watch for vertical development and note whether the high tops (anvil-shaped) are directly above the base or inclined more to the left or right. If they're inclined right, the squall is going right (so sail to the left to avoid it) and vice versa. If it's getting taller and darker and lined-up straight then it's coming directly at you.

THE OTHER TYPE of common squall is the line squall. These are less easy to avoid because, well, there's a line of them. But they too are often short-lived, despite their ominous look as they get closer and closer. Apart from the wall-to-wall line, these types of squalls are distinguished by causing all the local sea birds to fly away as, like you, they can't fly around the line. You can't fly with them so you've got three choices—

- plow on into it and get through it more quickly,
- heave-to so as to stay pretty much where you are, or
- sail away to reduce the apparent wind and have the gusts and waves on your quarter rather than crashing over your bows.

IF THE SQUALL seems especially severe, it might be best to roll up the genoa and fire up the engines to keep the boat pointed as close to the wind as possible, feathering the main to basically hold your position until the squall passes.

When either one of these squalls gets close to you (about one mile away) you'll first notice a 10-20% increase in wind speed. This will happen before it starts to rain.

Some squalls come as isolated events

Then the rain will commence—lightly if you're on the periphery of the squall and it's giving you just a glancing blow. If you find yourself in the direct path of an isolated squall or in the inevitable way of an advancing line squall it'll soon begin to rain hard and visibility will go down to hundreds of feet or even just a boat length.

Make sure you have located your rain gear and a mask or swim goggles. The enhanced wind velocity and driving rain makes looking into the face of the squall painful and difficult otherwise. Ask everyone not essential to the sailing of the catamaran to step into the saloon—they'll stay dry and warm, and out of the working crew's way.

Turn on your navigation lights and post a dedicated lookout.

STRATEGY VS TACTICS

No matter what theoretical or recommended strategy you read about and planned on taking (or that you practiced on your bareboat sailing course), the practical tactic you actually choose depends on the situation and on the skills of the crew.

If you have time, reef your mainsail.

- Check the deck and get rid of any cushions or loose items that might blow away.
- Check the painter of your dinghy if it's being towed (though it should be in davits). And check the lines you rigged to prevent the dinghy from swinging if in davits.
- Check kayaks and other toys so they don't blow off the boat.

NOTE: *If you are in the line of an oncoming squall, record your lat/lon position from the chart plotter to mark on your paper chart.*

If you've brought your handheld GPS unit, fetch it and get it working—a lightning strike is always a risk in a squall and there is a chance your boat electronics could be affected. You'll need to track course and speed (from the compass and by estimate) and plot them on your chart—or use the information to create a dead reckoning position. You'll need to know where you are in relation to land.

YOUR CHARTER YACHT is unlikely to have radar or a radar reflector and while you may be a mile or two offshore, there could be ferries and other power craft in the vicinity. You might be traveling 2-3 knots even if you're hove-to—so put your nav lights on and keep a lookout.

19

Heaving-To

PARK + RIDE IT OUT

Virtually every sailor who has received formal instruction learns the same things, since virtually every sailing school teaches the same skills: tacking, jibing, points of sail, sail trim, man overboard recovery, and heaving-to. These are the basics for any sailing education. Of all these skills, the one that tends to get forgotten is the last. Heaving-to isn't a throwaway skill, though, it's an essential tool.

This maneuver is so useful in so many ways that it should become a reflex action for every sailor. It is used for managing a quick passing squall, as a component of the Man Overboard (MOB) sequence, as a way to gain a respite from rough conditions, as an occasion for crew to grab some sleep and a host of other things—in fact, for any time the vessel needs to be brought to a controlled stop while still under way.

When hove-to, bear in mind that you are still sailing and you have the rights and responsibilities of the tack that you hove-to on—so all things being equal, starboard tack is preferred.

After the maneuver is completed, you'll be crabbing forward and sideways (leeward) at 1 to 2 knots. This sideways component creates a drift slick upwind that helps break up the waves approaching from that direction.

THE DOWNSIDE of this crabbing is that your boat will still be moving to leeward, so make sure that you have enough sea room in that direction. When heaving-to in order to get some rest or to prepare lunch—or even visit the 'seat of ease' in the throne room. Make sure you have at least 3 nautical miles of open water between you and the nearest land mass —or even the smallest shoal area.

There are two ways to heave-to. Your choice will depend on the direction in which you want your boat to drift. Decide which tack you need to be on, based on available sea room and the general direction you want to be going.

HERE'S HOW:

Let's say you've been beating hard upwind on a port tack in 4-to-6ft. seas, no reef in your sails, the wind about 16 knots. You're the only one on board able to steer and you want to take a break. Or, you see a squall up ahead and you would be more comfortable waiting until it passes.

Here's the easiest way to heave to:

1. Sheet in the mainsail to its normal close-hauled position— at, or a little below, the centerline.
2. Tack the boat, without releasing the headsail. Ensure the jib is trimmed in hard since you want to backwind the headsail. If you have a self-tacking headsail, set the stop on the track to keep the sail pinned to windward. Make the initial tack a bit slower than usual. Head into the wind but without passing through it, until the speed has really come down, before finishing the tack.
3. Once through the tack, ease the main since, if there is a

stiff breeze (as is often the case when heaving-to), the wind flowing over the main may create enough power and weather helm to push the bow back through the tack.

4. When you have completed tacking, you'll now be on a starboard tack. Your main has switched sides (as normal) and is now on port side, but your headsail hasn't swapped sides and is now set against the wind with its clew held to windward instead of leeward as usual. This is what is meant by a backed headsail.

5. To finish, turn your steering wheel all the way to windward and lock it by either fastening the center locking nut or by tying the wheel off with a length of small line.

To make things clear, since you are now on a starboard tack,

- turn your wheel all the way to starboard.
- The wind is now pushing the backed jib to leeward—to port in this case.
- The rudders are trying to steer the vessel to starboard. These opposed forces allow the vessel to settle into a stable state, neither under sail nor simply adrift.
- Use the mainsail to control the angle the boat is making to the wind. By trimming in the main, the boat will point higher, easing the main will let the bow fall off. Find the comfortable point you'd like to be on—if you wish to create a slick to windward, you might need to ease the mainsheet most of the way out and go beam-to the seas— or even drop the main altogether. If you are rolling too much, trim the main to point your bow a little more into the swell.

Simple enough. If you started from close-hauled, you probably didn't have to touch the sails at all. But what if you can't tack?

This may be because there's not enough sea room in that direction, or because crabbing that way will take you too far from where you want to go. There is another way to heave-to that keeps you on the same tack.

ASSUMING AGAIN that you're on port tack, here are the steps on a boat with a 'classic' headsail:

1. Take all of the slack out of the lazy headsail sheet (taking care to make sure that it's not snagged on a hatch or on anything at the mast).
2. Wrap four turns around its winch drum, then into the self-tailing jaws and insert the winch handle.
3. While continuing to steer at the same angle to the wind, ease and then release the working headsail sheet that's to leeward, while grinding-in on the hitherto lazy windward one.
4. Keep grinding the headsail to windward until the clew gets past the mast. How far aft you grind it will depend on the boat you're on and the size of your headsail. On all boats, grind the sail in until it's stretched fairly flat.
5. Once your headsail is successfully backed, proceed as above.

Your boat speed will already have diminished so all you need do is turn the wheel slowly all the way to windward—to oppose the pressure of the headsail. If you have a steering lock that works, apply it now. If you don't have a lock or it doesn't grip properly, lash the wheel with whatever line you have. We use the tail end of the windward jib sheet wound between the wheel and the windward winch —you won't even need a knot—just wrap it around the top of the self-tailing winch.

Once hove-to, the boat will have settled down; the pounding of the waves has greatly diminished and the boat is slowly moving and drifting in a smooth and comfortable manner, between 60-80° off the wind, depending on how much you eased the mainsail.

Not all boats react the same way when hove-to, so we suggest you practice in smooth waters with moderate winds before doing it in earnest.

> **NOTE**: *Some catamarans have forward-facing struts on the mast that make this maneuver hazardous to the headsail. Check with your briefer.*

OTHER USES FOR THE HEAVE-TO:

Heaving-to can be useful for reefing (or dropping) the main. In fact, if conditions are rough or you don't have an autopilot, heaving-to whilst reefing comes in pretty handy.

On a relatively calm day, when you want to have lunch without taking the time to douse sail and anchor or find a mooring—and conditions permit—heaving-to can be very pleasant, and lets the helmsman enjoy the meal at leisure. When boarding people from the dinghy—if you took them out sailing whilst others went ashore in the little boat; or there was no mooring ball available at a National Park snorkeling area—it makes getting the crew back on board a snap.

UNDOING THE HEAVE-TO:

Just as there are two ways to get into it, there are two ways to get out of being hove-to.

As before, the method you choose will depend on which tack/direction you want to resume heading—-and whether you've classic jib or a self-tacker.

Let's say you tacked into the heave-to and you now want to resume your earlier tack or course:

UNLOCK/UNLASH your wheel.

1. Turn it all the way to the other side. You will commence to fall off the wind and jibe the yacht.
2. You may need to ease the main out a little to help the boat turn—but make sure to trim it in again as you pass the stern through the wind—and then re-adjust both sails after you find the opposite tack.
3. The boat will jibe through a complete 270° turn and you will find yourself back on the same port tack you were on before the beginning of the maneuver.
4. Or, you can fire up the leeward engine and drive the boat onto the tack you've chosen.

IF YOU BACKED your headsail by grinding it to windward, here's how you get out of the heave-to:

1. Unlock/unlash the wheel.
2. Take the slack out of the leeward headsail sheet, making sure that it's not snagged anywhere at the mast or on deck, and load up four wraps and put it into the self-tailing jaws.
3. While continuing to steer at the same angle to the wind, first ease and then release the windward headsail sheet while grinding in on the leeward one.
4. If you've a self-tacking jib, this technique of getting out of heave-to isn't recommended as the stopper holding back the jib will be under load and difficult/dangerous to release.
5. Better to fire-up your engine for a minute and 'power tack' out of the heave-to or jibe out of it as described above.

Then re-adjust the stopper on the jib track when it is
unloaded.

NOTE: *Perform these maneuvers as slowly and gently as possible —quickly throwing the boat around increases apparent wind and can overpower the sail plan in breezy conditions.*

20

MOB Rules

DON'T GO OVERBOARD

The question of what to call the person in the water has colored much of the discussion of how best to retrieve them. Whether it's a man, woman, child or crew, the correct terminology is probably *Person*—but Man Over Board is still the most common expression for this circumstance in the English-speaking nautical world. And MOB is what the label on your chart-plotter's emergency button will say. So we'll stick with those.

In reality, perhaps the person most likely to fall overboard is the most qualified sailor on the vessel—namely, the skipper. Because if anything does go awry on the foredeck, a fouled jib sheet, say, it'll be they who'll likely hand the helm to someone else or press Auto and go forward to free it.

Things tend to go awry on the foredeck on days that are not mild and windless and calm, of course, but days that are rough and riotous. On such a day, the skipper could easily find himself in the drink with the yacht—and less experienced crew—sailing merrily on. If the boat is sailing at a conservative 6 knots, in one minute it'll be 200 yards/meters away.

Could they find the swimmer at that distance…let alone turn the ship around and pick him up in 15-20 knots of wind.?

NOTE: *A quick way to calculate speed and distance is known as:*

The 3-Minute Distance-Run Rule

Speed (kts)*100=Distance (yards or meters) run in 3 minutes

Example: Speed of 6 kts gives distance run in 3 minutes 6*100=600 yds/meters or, in 1 minute, 200 yds/meters.

SAILING INSTRUCTORS ARE TAUGHT to impart the time-honored Figure 8 and the more modern Quickstop techniques that are required in most of the different sailing certifications. They get fairly adept at demonstrating them after years of practice doing drills, week in and week out. When you've practiced a routine hundreds of times on different boats and in different sea conditions, it's pretty easy to execute a perfect save using either of these two techniques under sail alone. Find them on the Links page on our web site.

DURING THE TYPICAL week-long sailing course, a dedicated and well-taught student can usually demonstrate a save—albeit under fairly artificial conditions (they've been reading about it, studying the diagrams in the books, seeing it demonstrated by the instructor, seeing other students have a go, having crew mates who are expecting to serve in their designated roles, etc.). But this is not how things will be in real life.

In that circumstance, it will likely have been years since you last took your course and you probably haven't practiced it every year like the instructor suggested. The crew may not have been on that course and don't know the drill. Crew may get distracted by the tense commotion in the cockpit, or lose sight of a white shirt among the whitecaps. And did we mention the confusion the MOB might be feeling as the boat hurtles away into the distance?

So what to do? First, relax. There is a pretty much foolproof way of getting someone back on board—one that is simple to learn and easy to execute.

IF YOU'RE from the US or are well-versed in telecom companies, you'll be familiar with *AT&T*. Use it as a handy acronym to remember what to do should you ever find yourself called to action:

Assign a spotter. Have them stand or sit high in a secure manner somewhere where you can see them. Instruct the spotter them to point an extended arm at the MOB so you know where they are in relation to the boat. This way you only have to look at the spotter and not frantically crane your neck to look for the MOB yourself.

- The spotter must never take their eyes off the MOB or try to help in any other way--because the instant they lose sight of the swimmer it can be difficult to reestablish visual contact. And they must continue to point in the direction of the MOB without distraction. So don't give this person another job to do!
- At this stage, you could also press the MOB function on your chart plotter but know that is just the 'ground' position and the victim will be drifting in wind-generated current. But it will serve as a decent reference point if visual contact is lost.
- Throw something floaty. The horseshoe or round lifebelt (PFD) that will be attached to the lifelines or guardrails close to the cockpit is ideal but it's sometimes fiddly to detach—so chuck some cockpit cushions as well. They should be easier to get to and large enough to see. Throw anything else that floats—cushions, life jackets, fenders — anything that will create a visual reference. You can always retrieve them later.

- Tack. And we don't mean a regular tack where you throw off one jib sheet and pull in another as part of a smooth coordinated operation. We mean a Crash Tack.

NOTE: If the cat you are on has a self-tacking jib, with a track running across the beam of the boat, it's critical to move the jib track stop to windward **before doing the crash tack**. If you don't, the power of the unbacked jib will mess-up the maneuver and leave the MOB still swimming.

- Tell your crew in a LOUD and FIRM manner what you are about to do. Especially warn the spotter, since they must keep their eyes on the MOB whilst the boat rapidly changes direction—the swimmer might end up on the opposite side of the boat, and the spotter has to be able to see them at all times. And if you've got a self-tacking jib, have someone quickly move the stopper on the track to prevent the jib from sliding over as it would normally do in a tack.
- Throw the helm over until you've tacked somewhere past close-hauled (say 60 degrees to the wind)--but don't release the jib. To make sure this doesn't happen by dint of sheer habit, tell your crew to not release or touch any jib sheets as you tack. This will cause the jib to back—that is, be on the windward side of where it normally lies, and countering the pull of the mainsail.
- Once the jib has backed (it'll take just a second or two) and the boat has lost almost all of its forward momentum, swing the wheel over in the opposite direction as if tacking, to counter the turning force of the headsail. For example, if the jib is trying to push the boat to the left, apply full right rudder. Provided you've lost most of your speed (which happens within about five seconds on most bareboats) the boat will not tack back.
- Lock, lash, or just press your thigh to the wheel to keep it in place.

- You are now hove-to—your boat is moving slowly forwards and sideways (leeward) at 1-2 knots in most conditions.
- Check for any lines dangling in the water—dinghy painter especially—and immediately **start your engines**. If you've left them in reverse to stop the prop from spinning, put the shifter back in neutral first (if you forget to do this, don't worry—the engine will start anyway with no damage and a bit of reverse will only help proceedings).
- Apply as many bursts of forward or reverse thrust as necessary on alternate engines to bring the lee side of the boat toward the victim. The key idea here is to use your engines to counter the forward component of your drift, leaving the sideways (wind-driven) component to bring you alongside your recently overboard crew member.
- Aim to pick up near the stern, avoiding the risk of contact with the spinning propeller by shifting into neutral. Be careful that the boat isn't being blown down over the floating MOB. When within range, toss them a life ring or even a fender (attached to a line, of course). That way they'll have some support, and crew can pull them closer to the boat.
- And be careful of the prop! The catamaran's propellers are quite close to the surface. The MOB may be exhausted from the effort of staying afloat in wet clothing--as well as distraught (if not totally freaked out) by the experience. There's a risk their legs could drift beneath the boat, exposing them to the propeller, so position the victim clear of the prop and make sure the transmission stays in neutral.
- Once the victim is alongside and the transmission in neutral, throw them a line or have them climb up the swim ladder, if they're fit enough. Help them maneuver to the transom of the boat close to the ladder.

THEY MAY NEED assistance to get out of the water, so appoint crew to stand by and help. If there's any swell, the boat will be pitching up and down and the swim ladder may quickly become a hazard. There should be several crew available to grab an arm or try to get a length of dock line around the victim to help pull them up.

Get them out of wet clothes and/or wrap a towel around them to prevent hypothermia. The combination of a stiff breeze and a wet body can reduce body temperature rapidly, even in the tropics.

If the swim ladder isn't an option, tie a large bowline in a dock line and have the victim slip the line over their head and under the armpits. Tie the free end to a spare halyard and gently winch the MOB out of the water. If possible, slacken the lifelines so it's easier to get them on board.

WHEN IT IS time to get out of the heave-to, first raise the swim ladder. Make sure there are no lines dangling overboard, then free and center your wheel.

Practice makes perfect, so try it out at least once during your charter. It only takes a few minutes and will give you peace of mind. A wind-blown hat going over the side makes the best practice as it happens as unexpectedly as a real MOB.

Have the crew practice the drill alternating the person at the helm. After all, the MOB could be any one of you!

WHY NOT JUST GET IN the **RIB** *dinghy?*

1. First, it is most likely in davits. Launching into a turbulent sea is no easy task. And, if in davits, it may not have its motor attached, since on some cats the dinghy motor can drag through the rooster tail streaming from between the hulls at high speed. In St Martin and some other

Caribbean bases, the charter companies insist that the dinghy engine be lifted and placed on the boat's dedicated pad on the pushpit, or stern rail.

2. Second, getting into the dinghy in open water can be a challenging business—the dinghy may be bouncing around in chop, for example. The dinghy's engine may not start first time and in your rush to try, you may flood it. Or, someone may enthusiastically release the painter and send you drifting. And can you see the victim now that you're lower to water level?

CAN you handle a RIB in waves? Get the victim back in a dinghy? It's not as easy as it seems—especially when the victim is fully clothed.

Then there's the dinghy propeller, which is just inches below the surface. Props and people are not a good combination.

So, *No* to the dinghy. *Yes* to practicing the MOB maneuver. It's a fundamental part of a sailor's repertoire. Hopefully you'll never have to utilize it—most sailors have spent years on the water and never had to experience a real MOB. But someday it'll happen—maybe to you. Best be ready.

21

Hooking Down
ANCHOR WITH CONFIDENCE

At some point, you're going to want to change rhythm and stop sailing. After first prepping the crew on the upcoming procedures and having dropped sail and tidied up the deck, you may be ready to stop for lunch or overnight in one of the secluded bays and coves that bejewel the Caribbean.

In which case you'll want to anchor. Or it may be that you arrived too late to get a mooring ball—or the only mooring ball left looks a bit dubious. Then you're going to *have* to anchor.

It's not so hard—all you're really doing is dropping onto the seabed a heavy metallic object that won't move, with a line tied to it that is attached to the boat. There are a few variables—where you drop the anchor, how much cable you put out in how much water, and so on. But really, how hard can it be? (*Cue riotous laughter!*).

Well, actually it's pretty simple if you take your time—it may take up to half an hour or more to get the boat properly settled on the hook—and do it carefully.

And let us say right up front—never be afraid to pull up the anchor and reset it if you're not entirely satisfied with your position. It won't take all that long and the peace of mind will be well worth the extra effort. Sometimes it just means dropping the anchor 10 yards/meters further ahead or a bit to the side.

THOSE SMALL CHANGES can have a large impact on how the boat lies to the wind and how much space you have around you. We have happily reset our anchor several times before we were satisfied—mostly when we expected a big blow to head our way, but sometimes just to avoid coming too close to a neighbor. It's no fun to be eating dinner with your neighbor sitting within earshot—especially when you're listening to some uplifting choral music and they're head-banging like crazy. Or vice versa!

PREPARING TO ANCHOR:

First, check the supplied cruising guide and supplementary charter company notes, which will tell you whether any anchoring restrictions apply. If you see no other boats anchored, ask yourself what might be the reason? You could be the first person to arrive at a less frequently visited bay—or you might be trying to anchor in an untenable or notoriously dangerous spot.

YOUR CHART MAY HAVE *anchor* (as well as *no anchoring*) symbols but your cruising guide will have much more detailed and useful information on the best spot to anchor in the bay of your choice. It'll tell you the water depth and—just as important—the nature of the seabed and what's ashore. If the bay you fancy isn't mentioned in the cruising guide, there may be a good reason why not—so don't assume that you're the first to discover a brilliant new spot.

Then again, just because it's not mentioned doesn't mean it's not a viable possibility. There are many very good anchorages that are only suitable for one or two boats at a time—and sometimes the authors of the guidebooks may have chosen to keep some spots a secret. But don't be too bold about dropping the hook in an unfamiliar and undocumented spot—it might be a very bad decision.

NEXT, assess the all-important wind direction. Although the general wind direction in the Caribbean is from the east (more NE in winter, more SE in summer) the wind direction where you're anchoring may be quite different—maybe even 180 degrees different.

This is because most island anchorages are on the sheltered, leeward side of a headland or other body of land. The eddies this land creates can cause the local winds to vary from the general pattern.

If you're the first or only boat in your bay of choice, you'll have to figure this out yourself, but often someone is there ahead of you.

Aside from being an obstacle to avoid, this vessel is serving as your local direction indicator for how you'll need to align your boat before dropping your hook. If there are several boats, choose the one nearest where you plan to drop.

Generally, catamarans and power yachts lie differently to the wind than deeper-keeled monohulls so, if there's a conflict, align with the boat that's more like the one you're on. And if the direction that the boats lie is unrelated to the local wind, that might indicate some current—which, while generally slight, may be significant twice a month—at times of full and new moon.

> **NOTE**: *Sometimes there are both wind and current in an anchorage or mooring field but the direction that the boats closest to you are pointing is always the direction of that combined wind and current.*

IF you have to anchor close behind another boat, don't be afraid to motor up very close to their stern. Drop the hook a few feet behind —say 10 feet or less—and you'll fall back safely and snug up. In the morning, if you need to weigh anchor before the boat in front is ready to move, they will probably motor ahead by a boat length or so to give you room to maneuver. If they've left the boat and gone to dive or hike on land, you can pull up close, with anchor cable reeled in and, after snubbing the chain, motor astern and drag the anchor free.

Or, use your dinghy to nudge the other boat to one side for a few minutes whilst you pull the hook. These latter techniques may also come in handy after a wind or current shift, or if someone anchors after you and has fallen back to float above your anchor.

OVERALL, though, the most important factor when anchoring is to give yourself plenty of time. Arriving late to an anchorage and being obliged to find a spot before the sunlight disappears is often an anxiety-inducing situation.

> **NOTE**: *Plan your afternoon arrival before you begin sailing each day. Work backwards, setting waypoints to indicate the passage of time—and give yourself an absolute deadline to make sure you get to the anchorage in good daylight. It may sound excessive, but you'll find the sun sets around 1800 hrs in the middle of winter (aka high season). And in the tropics, the sun goes down like flipping a switch. In 20 minutes everything's dark.*

UPON ARRIVAL at your chosen destination, if you don't feel comfortable about your options, then move to another anchorage. Plan to arrive no later than 1500 hours (3:00pm). You need the sun to be still somewhat high in the sky—and remember the sun sets around 1750-1900 (5:50-7:00pm). In some bays, you'll be anchoring in 15-20', enabling you to see the bottom in order to drop your anchor in the light-colored sand rather than the darker sea grass. At other times you'll be in deeper water, up to 30', and not able to see the bottom clearly.

Check your cruising guide to ensure your chosen spot is a safe one for overnight anchoring and proceed in the knowledge that it's been tried and tested by boats with older, less secure anchors than you've got on board your modern bareboat with its new pattern, quick-setting anchor.

SCOPE IT OUT:

The general rule of thumb for anchoring usually advises a 5-to-1 scope for chain and 7-to-1 for line. In the Caribbean you'll have mostly chain anchor cable with possibly a few feet of nylon attached to the chain locker fitting. So if you want a number, go with 4 times the depth **measured from the bow-roller** as a minimum. Bear in mind that some charter companies calibrate their depth-sounders to show depth under the keel rather than the actual depth from below water level. (Check with your Boat Briefer before departing). The bow roller may be a good 2 meters or more above the water line.

POINT THE BOAT head-to-wind or current as indicated by nearby boats, in order to drift the boat to a stop at the right spot. Use a short blast of reverse if you have to.

On a catamaran you'll be able to hold the boat steady with your two engines—but drop the hook straight away. Do this using the anchor windlass remote control or by using a winch handle to release the windlass clutch. The windlass will drop the hook slowly (about one foot per second/1 meter every 3 seconds) but using the clutch release will send it down like the lump of metal it is.

IN A STIFF BREEZE you're much better off using the clutch release to drop your hook—even though you'll hold the boat fairly straight into the wind, your vast amount of windage will still push the cat around. When dropping the anchor by easing the windlass clutch, be extra careful not to catch vulnerable fingers and other parts in the machinery.

WINDLASS CLUTCH QUICK DROP:

Allow the wind to push the boat's bows back and away while letting out more chain—whilst applying power to either engine to keep the boat straight into the wind. Make sure you don't give too much power to the engines because you might end up holding a stationary position—rather than falling back—and drop your chain in one big pile on the seabed rather than stretching it out. Use short bursts on the throttle rather than a prolonged application of power. Look 90 degrees sideways and make a transit with two in-line objects to check your movement.

Most bareboats have 50 meters (164') of chain spliced to 10 meters (33') of nylon. You don't really want to use the nylon unless you have to, so 30' of water depth is pretty much your limit for safe overnight anchoring, assuming a well-set anchor in good holding ground.

But you shouldn't need to push this limit since catamarans draw so much less than monohulls and you'll be able to drop your hook in waters that monohulls can't venture. Just be careful that you have enough swing room should the wind direction do a 180-degree shift as can occasionally happen during the passing of an isolated squall.

UNLIKE MOORING BALLS, whose swing radius is defined by your boat length plus your mooring bridle (and dinghy plus its painter), when anchored you'll be swinging around what's known as the lift point—the point at which your chain lifts off the seabed toward your bow.

The stronger the wind and/or current, the closer the lift point will move toward your anchor and the greater your swing radius will be. If you're anchored close to similar boats, with similar length of chain out, then you should all swing together and stay separated.

Problems arise when you're near a boat with a profile different from your own. If you're next to a monohull they will have more boat in the water than out of it while your profile will be reversed and so you will swing more readily to the wind than they. This is a good reason to stay as separated as you can to start with, and also try to anchor near boats like yours. And, of course, the catamaran needs less water depth than the monohull, generally speaking.

MANY BAREBOATS HAVE POORLY MARKED anchor cables, making it tricky to judge how much chain you have out. Since you'll almost always have more chain out of the boat than in it, one simple way is to open up the anchor locker and estimate how much chain you have left.

If you know that the boat has 160-odd feet (the standard 50 meters most bare boats have) and it looks like you've got 20 feet left, then you have 140' out. Or, you could make your own marks in the chain with brightly colored cable ties (aka zip-ties) if you've had the foresight to bring them with you.

NOTE: *Another rough formula for the average 45' boat is: "Boat length plus double the depth" as applying the often-cited 4-5 times the depth would often not be enough at the shallower depths Caribbean bareboaters are restricted to.*

For example, at 10 ft water depth (found off Anegada, BVI) 45 ft plus 20 comes out at 65' (while simply 5 x 10' depth would have you let out just 50 ft. When in doubt, let more out—(provided you have swing room.)

THE POWER SET:

This technique both ensures that the anchor is set in good holding ground and helps set it a bit deeper. The key is to first let the natural forces of wind and current do their job for a minute or two while sighting two fixed objects (one near, one further away) at right angles to you, known as a Transit Bearing. Then put the engines into reverse (with the wheel centered and locked or lashed) at the lowest possible revs (usually 900/1,000 rpm).Make sure the clutch on your windlass is tightened up, or the locking safety plate (on boats that have one, of course) is in place. Gradually increase the rpm until you are holding tight at around 1,500. Keep your eye on the transit, making sure the two elements stay in line.

ONCE THE POWER Set has proved that your anchor is holding, rig your bridle/snubber line (the chain hook or shackle attached to lines leading to the forward end of each hull) to take the pressure off the windlass. Rigging this hook around a link in the chain can be tricky, since you often have to slide a hand and forearm through a small slot to access the chain, so be patient. And be aware of the dangers of catching exposed body parts as the boat yaws around the tight chain.

When the bridle hook is in place, the resulting pivot point will be quite a bit forward of your bows and quite low to the water.

GPS ANCHOR ALARMS are useless here as you are so close to rocks and other boats that the sound of them rubbing against your hull will wake you up before your alarm goes off. Not to mention the likelihood of losing your GPS fix momentarily during the night—a constant occurrence—will mean a false alarm in the wee small hours.

Assemble and raise an anchor ball if you've got one on board. This black plastic folding signal shows—in daylight—that you're anchored, not underway. At sunset, turn on your anchor light (white all-round light at top of mast) but don't forget to turn it off in the morning. If, as is sometimes the case, the masthead light isn't working, try and make do with the steaming light and a cockpit light—that way you'll have a 360 degree white light showing, as required. It's not perfect but it's better than nothing.

Don't turn on your red and green running lights—although many sailors do—unless you are actually underway. It sends a dangerously confusing signal to other vessels.

Raise the anchor ball.

NOTE: *Some sailors scoff at the anchor ball, thinking it a needless complication. These are sailors who haven't been run into by a rum-sozzled pirate in the middle of the day. The lack of an anchor ball might well void any insurance claim.*

ANCHORING ETIQUETTE:

The first boat in an anchorage sets the style for all other arrivals. If the first one decides to anchor close to shore and put a stern line onto the beach so as not to swing, then all others anchoring close by are expected to do likewise.

If that first boat decides to swing freely to a single anchor, then the next boat can't decide to anchor bow and stern and thus impede boat #1. It's not a law of the sea, but it's definitely the rule of the anchorage. Unless, of course, boat #1 is a 20-foot weekender and boat #2 is a 60-foot motor yacht. Then the Law of Tonnage applies. Woe betide anyone who disregards it!

The best advice is to get to your anchorage early in the afternoon so you have ample time to pick your spot and to check your anchor by snorkeling over it to ensure it is set.

WHEN THE NEW arrival is too close for your comfort, there is the makings of a delicate situation. On one hand, you don't want to be a total *Asterisk* by loudly demanding their immediate departure. On the other, it's not as if he's parked too close at the mall and you have to squirm your way out of the driver's seat—the danger is he might drag down on you in a 40-knot squall and break some stanchions, if not pull out your anchor with his.

IF YOU ARE CONCERNED about the way your new neighbor is anchoring, convey that information as quickly and clearly—and gently—as possible. Why let him drop an anchor, lay out chain and go through all the rituals that anchoring demands and then have you announce,

'I say, aren't you a tad too close, Sir?'

No—stand up and wave him away at first opportunity, though with sensitivity of course.

ANCHORING IN A TIGHT CORNER, we once had a French voyager shout passionately, 'I have 100 meters of chain. 100 METERS! I swing you all night!'

Not wishing to be swung all night by a florid Frenchman, we moved away. (Though if he really did have 100 meters out, had he swung to port he'd be 20 meters up the beach, and on the other swing he'd be stuck on the reef, but never mind.)

THINGS NEEDN'T BE SO confrontational, however. Follow these steps if a boat motors up to you while you're relaxing in the shady cockpit on your own securely anchored boat. They signify escalating concern:

1. Look up from your coffee/tea/beverage
2. Give helmsperson a hard stare (as in don't even think about it).
3. Stand up with hard stare.
4. Walk to a point on your deck closest to offending boat (still with hard stare).
5. Fold arms (elevate hard stare to Evil Eye)
6. Place hands on your hips (arms akimbo).

Nothing need be said until this stage is reached. Most newbie bareboaters (even newbie boat owners) are unsure of their anchoring skills and will be looking nervously around at every boat close to them.

Often, the new arrival is so concerned about their anchoring procedures that they don't take enough notice of the neighbors—things may seem settled at that moment but how will it be if a squall rolls through and spins all the boats 90 degrees?

Most will get the idea that they're too close by Step 3 and will decide to move further away. If they persist in anchoring too close (by your definition—not theirs) then resist getting into a shouting match.

Instead, dinghy yourself over and politely point out that you're uncomfortable with their position as it's too close. All but the most belligerent sailor will reluctantly agree and move further off. You could even offer to help them based on your own newfound expertise—and so make a new friend!

IF ANOTHER BOAT does anchor close to you and the skipper shows no interest in honoring your entreaties, no matter how subtle or broad, sometimes the only option is to move away yourself. If this looks like being the case, put all your fenders on the vulnerable side.

Or at the last resort, plan your move carefully since the anchorage is no doubt filling up.

Don't leave it too late. If you are not able to move, deploy your fenders all around the vessel in case your neighbors end up dragging in the night. If you are truly concerned about weather and dragging, set an anchor watch overnight—schedule crew on a rotating 3-hour watch from 2100 until sunrise.

OR, if the situation requires drastic action, stand at the rail and bellow, 'I have 100 meters of chain. 100 METERS. I swing you all night.' Accent optional.

It's rather effective.

22

Pickup Artistry
PLAY BALL

Showtime!

The mooring field is one of the two main theaters where: Sometimes you watch the show, or

Sometimes you are the show.

Before you get to enjoy watching the show from the comfort of your catamaran's comfortable lounges, you and your crew will have already performed for the audience that got there ahead of you. So be sure to give them a good show (and by that, we mean showing the crowd how picking up a mooring should be done).

When picking up a mooring, the thing to keep in mind is our motto: Slow is Pro. Make it your mantra. Our tips for a drama-free perfect pick-up:

Moorings in the Caribbean consist of mainly two types,

1. Proper Mooring balls, and
2. The Rest—Free-floating lines with a float attached, such as a bleach bottle or a detergent jug.

PROPER MOORING BALLS are associated with the better-managed anchorages. These are moorings in which lines or cable are professionally laid. A chain or robust line leads from a sturdy sand screw or large concrete block up to a large plastic floating ball. You pay for them but you'll get a receipt from a real company and the knowledge that there's someone to go after in the unlikely event the mooring fails.

The Rest are none of the above. Choose Wisely!

THE LINES or cable attached to a proper mooring ball are of two types:

1. The downline: Rope or chain which drops vertically to the seabed from the floating plastic ball. This chain is attached to a concrete block or an eye drilled into the rock or screwed into the sand, and
2. The pennant (or pendant): This is attached to the downline at the fitting on the floating plastic ball and floats free on the water, waiting to be picked up and attached to a cleat aboard ship. Often, the pennant will have a small plastic float attached to keep the eye floating on the surface, so aim to hook the pennant and not the float.

This eye is at the free end of the pennant and usually has a plastic or metal fitting within it. This fitting makes it difficult to simply slip the eye over a cleat, so please don't try.

THE PROPER WAY TO attach the mooring pennant is

1. By attaching a line (almost always a dock line) to a cleat and leading it, clear of all obstructions, to the pennant.

2. Then passing it through the eye and leading it back to the cleat it started from, so both ends of the line are attached to the same cleat.

3. The line can be first attached by tying a bowline in one end and passing the loop of that knot through the base of the cleat and over the horns.

4. If the base is too narrow and can't accommodate the loop being pushed through, just tie a bowline through the base and cleat-hitch the returning end.

5. Or, simply attach the line by way of a cleat hitch, then lead it through the eye of the mooring pennant, then back to the cleat—where you can tie another cleat hitch atop the first.

Do the same on the opposite side, so you have two looped lines. One running starboard-starboard and the other port-port.

Simply leading a single line from port to starboard will allow the vessel to slide along its length creating chafe and causing wide swings in gusty weather.

ON SOME CATS, the mooring lines are led from cleats attached to the cross beam at the bows. On others, they are led from cleats on the outside of each hull. Yet other models have special cleats attached to the inside edge of each hull. Make sure your deck crew inspect the yacht and check with your boat briefer to see which applies to you.

WHEN APPROACHING THE MOORING BALL, these port and starboard lines should each already be attached at one end, with the free end led first outside the vessel beneath the deck railings, then laid back over the same railings in readiness. Much depends on the wind conditions. In calm weather with a small breeze, it is a simple thing for the person driving the boat to motor up to place the mooring at the feet of the line handler. Charter catamarans come with a vast array of differing helm positions, so hand signals from one person on the foredeck may be essential to confirm the skipper's view.

Mooring lines led around outside of hull

At the crew's signal, the driver should apply a gentle burst of reverse to bring the vessel to a stop. The crew member can simply lean over and pluck the pennant from the surface with a boathook.

By using the throttles carefully, the driver can hold position while the deck crew thread the dock lines through the eye of the pennant and back to the appropriate cleats, either attached to the cross-beam or to the outside of each hull.

Look 90 degrees left or right to find a transit and make sure the boat is holding position so the line handlers can work their magic efficiently.

Two crew can work together and secure each line simultaneously. If you have only one able-bodied person to handle the lines, have them snug-up the first bridle as tightly as they can and temporarily cleat it off while they thread through the other one. At this stage, the driver can come forward and take out the slack on the second line as the crew working the bow position surges out the first until they're equal.

If you've got a reasonably able crew (of any age) you can easily teach them to thread the second line straight after the first and then lead them back together while the driver keeps the boat hovering on the spot.

In some extreme situations—inclement weather, missing boat hook —the smart thing might be to put your dinghy into the water and motor it around to the bow and pass up the pennant by hand!

> **NOTE:** *If you have been shown a different method by an experienced teacher on a different type of boat, and it still works for you on a big catamaran, by all means use it. There are so many variables in terms of freeboard and cleat placement among the various brands and sizes of charter cats—and they are changing constantly—that we will just stay with the tried and true.*

One habit of mooring balls is that when the wind drops, or local tide current changes, they sometimes tap against the hull, making an annoying sound for occupants of the forward cabins. Stop this by hauling on the mooring pennant so the ball is pulled clear of the water—it's the small chop and water movement caused by the change of tide or the wake of a passing dinghy that creates the tapping sound, so pulling the ball up removes it from these influences.

Remove the mooring line from the bridle and pull as tight as possible to prevent tapping against the hull.

If you forget to do this and get woken up in the night, just put in some earplugs or earbuds because by then there's nothing you can do about it and no harm will be done to the boat.

A simple way to check the health of the mooring line is to grab a face mask and fins and jump in the water. Follow the mooring line down to see that all parts are secure. The places to check are the shackles both beneath the mooring ball and at the bottom of the downline where it meets the sand screw or concrete block (watch for unsecured shackle screw pins), the top end of the downline (in case some cowboy has wrapped the line around their propeller).

SUCH ISSUES ARE rare these days but, in the (approximate) words of the great Captain Ron: *"If it's going to happen, it'll happen out there."*

The most likely time to find these anomalies is at the end of the busy charter season when the moorings have been given a stressful months-long workout. If you have any doubts, try for a better mooring. Check most thoroughly in those favorite snorkel spots that attract hundreds of boats per week and are a must-stop on everyone's itinerary.

RECENTLY, some BVI destinations, such as Norman Island, have installed mooring balls where previously there had been none— Benures Bay, for example. This serves a two-fold purpose:

- It frees up the congested bays where anchoring is difficult (because of the water depth) but demand for the available moorings is high, and
- It allows sailors who aren't confident in their anchoring skills to enjoy the anchorages which were previously unavailable. And bear in mind that while a charter skipper might be quite capable of anchoring a boat, they may be nervous about doing so in extremely tight circumstances—preferring a mooring for the peace of mind it can offer.

These private balls are for advanced bookings only

And, in the BVI as well, since 2017 a company called BoatyBall has made it possible to reserve certain mooring balls in advance via a dedicated app.

23

Tie One Off

MOOR ASHORE

In some anchorages—particularly very deep ones—it can make sense to anchor with the vessel's stern close to the shore. Often you'll find that the water depth just a boat-length from shore might be 10 feet or more. It is often possible to get within a few feet of the shore and still be in a safe depth (and remember the tidal movement in the Caribbean may be only two feet, maximum).

It is not uncommon to see several yachts lined up next to each other, sterns tied off to trees on the shore. And remember that it is the first boat to anchor that sets the rule for the anchorage—you won't make any friends if you decide to sit swinging to anchor if you're in the middle of a group of boats anchored fore-and-aft, or with a stern line running ashore. Similarly, if the others are swinging on anchors, don't feel you can drop your hook in the middle of them and set a line ashore—eventually those boats are going to swing into you.

One way to check the suitability is to motor gently towards the shoreline, bow first. Set a hawk-eyed person on the bow to observe the seabed and look for hazards. As you approach, take note of the depths as displayed on your instruments—bearing in mind the depth transducer may be 10 feet aft of the bow.

Once satisfied where the limits of safe water might be, back out and find an appropriate spot to anchor so that the anchor is far enough out that it'll dig in—but not so far that you'll run out of cable before your stern gets close to the shore.

When you are satisfied that the anchor is well-set, use two, three, or four dock lines tied together to make up a long enough stern line. Bareboats don't come with long sets of line for this purpose. But avoid using the kedge anchor warp, since you still might need it as an auxiliary.

You could use the dinghy to get the line ashore, or, if you have a reasonably good swimmer on board, let them tie the stern line around their waist and swim it to the shore. Hold the boat in place by using gentle reverse thrust against your anchor whilst paying out the shore line to your swimmer.

Sometimes it will help if the swimmer attaches a fender or other float to the line's midpoint. The seabed can shelve up steeply just a few meters from shore. If the line sinks to the bottom, the extra weight of line in the water can make the swimmer's task harder than it need be. The float will keep the line on the surface, lessening its drag.

When your swimmer is ashore, they should tie the line around a sturdy rock or tree trunk, making sure it is free of obstructions. When we say rock we mean a big, thick substantial rock, not something you might be able to lift an inch off the ground by yourself. And by tree trunk we mean something too thick to be bent by a single person—or even a couple of people.

When tying the line around the rock or tree, the knot to use is the *Round Turn and Two Half-Hitches*. Why? Because you can untie it even under strain. Unlike, say, the bowline.

With the stern line(s) pulled back and made fast to your stern cleats (or headsail sheet winches), tighten them by pulling yourself forward a bit, using the anchor windlass to take up some of the cable.

You may need a second stern line as sometimes you might need to stop from moving too close to a similarly secured neighboring vessel. In tight quarters, cross the stern lines in an X shape to further stabilize the vessel.

Charter yachts at anchor with stern lines led ashore

When releasing the shore lines prior to departure, first let out a little anchor chain from the bow. This will create slack in the system sufficient to make loosening and then untying the shore lines a simple affair. Send someone ashore to release the lines from the tree or rock to which they've been attached, then use the final shore line to pull the crew back to the boat.

If there are still boats anchored close to you and with stern lines led ashore, use your engine in low reverse gear, stretching out the anchor cable, to keep from drifting into them. In stiff cross winds, you'll need to quickly reel yourself forward to get out of their way. If you think you may be getting too close, have the crew dangle fenders alongside, just in case.

Whilst this may seem a complicated business, it is really fairly simple. After having done it a couple of times, you'll be able to get the boat tied down quickly. You'll find you have created a great platform for swimming in the shallows, playing on the beach, and other joys that are a little more complicated when swinging at anchor. If you have young kids aboard, it makes for a nice private pool, as well.

24

Dock Approach
SLIP TIPS

E very year we see a number of world-girdling sailors pass through the islands. They are as salty and weather-beaten as you would wish, their vessels sometimes encrusted with oceanic growth, sometimes as pristine as a show-ring pony. They have covered many thousands of miles in all conditions; have beaten back the wrath of storms and endured days of windless ennui.

We have the utmost respect for these skillful sailors—they are out there, doing it. But whatever they have done in those many months, it's a good bet they haven't had to put their boat onto a busy dock very often.

NOW WE DON'T MEAN to disparage the skills of the long-distance sailor but we would point out that some of the best boat handling and docking you'll ever see is performed day-in and day-out by the dock staff at the big charter companies.

They may be challenged to navigate from there to the rum shop, but they'll back a 50-foot catamaran down a busy channel and into a slip without blinking. Because they do it every day.

'It's all right for the professionals,' you may say. But none of us were born naturals at docking and we all still occasionally make mistakes or misjudgments. We're often on different boats with different handling characteristics and have learned that the distance between perfection and an insurance claim is a mere few centimeters.

Judging speed, distance, and the actions of other boat operators is a skill that can be developed with experience and time, but you probably don't have a lot of either. The only way to truly perfect your docking technique is the same as with anything else: practice makes perfect. Even a little practice will improve your skill immensely.

CHECK these points for information on the factors that come into play as you dock a large cruising boat into a slip or onto a dock. These factors apply to all boats.

Before beginning any maneuvers, be aware that there might be one or more casual observers standing on the dock—perhaps waiting for a friend to pick them up in a dinghy, perhaps just wandering the docks to look at the pretty boats. They will be instantly attracted to your approaching vessel—finally, some action!

Pay them no mind. Keep your attention confined to your boat and others that might get in its way, the wind, the dock, the targets on the dock, and other items. Any distractions from bystanders—who may know something about what you are doing, but often have no clue at all—will be to the detriment of your work. So go ahead and keep your attention to things that directly impact your performance. Though if a bystander shouts, 'There's a puppy in the water,' you might pay heed!

DOCKING: Here are the main considerations when docking. Some you can control or at least be aware of and be able to factor into your decision-making. Others are factors beyond your control that you have to learn to work with or live with.

. . .

THINGS YOU CAN CONTROL:

1. **Rate of Turn**: On all boats, you can judge the rate of turn by seeing how quickly the boat's bows move against the background. Use the rolled-up jib or a stanchion as a reference. On a catamaran, it's often difficult—or impossible—to see all four corners from your helm station, so appoint a spotter to give you feedback as to distance off the dock, other boats, dinghy in the water, etc.

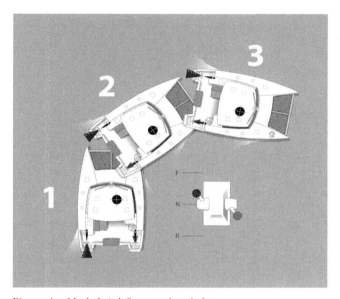

Pivot point (black dot) defines turning circle

2. **Arc of Turn**: When turning while going forward, try to focus not only on the movement of the bow. Don't forget that the stern is moving sideways, but in the opposite direction. The resultant arc is also affected by the fact that you are in a fluid and that the boat slides or crabs as it turns, like a car skidding sideways through a turn. Be aware that, going forward, the stern of one hull is on the outside of your turning circle while the bow of the opposite hull is

on the inside. It's the opposite going stern-first. In both cases, it's the pivot point of the boat that actually defines the circumference of your turning circle.

The wheel will be centered and locked and you'll be using only your engines to turn your boat in close quarters. You'll be able to spin a cat around in just over a boat length.

OTHER FACTORS:

Glide Zone: This is how far momentum will carry the boat forward or backward without any engine thrust. It will vary greatly depending on wind speed and direction—as well as your boat's own size, weight and speed when you engage neutral—and the cleanliness of the hulls!

Blades: Since some catamarans differ in their underwater layout, check whether the props are ahead of or behind the rudders. In most cases the rudder is aft of the propeller, in the usual way. When you engage forward gear, a flow of water from the propeller immediately rushes over the leading edge of your rudder which, unless the steering wheel is locked, will simply align itself with the flow.

If, however, the props on your cat are behind the rudders, no flow passes over the rudders in forward gear. In reverse, though, a rush of water is forced against the trailing edge of your rudder. Because the rudder posts are all closer to the rudders' leading edge, your rudders will slam against their stops to the right or left, unless the wheel is locked or held firm. These full-left or full-right rudders will not help your backward maneuvering in close quarters, and could suffer damage.

THE DOCK APPROACH:

Survey the dock. Are there any dock staff? Call on your VHF to ask permission or guidance from the dockmaster, particularly if picking up fuel or water (where there may be a wait). Do an initial pass-by to check out the space available. What's the dock height for your fenders? Are there cleats or bollards?

Consider the wind and the available maneuvering space; circle back around to the starting point you've chosen to begin your approach.

Looking at the dock, decide where you'd like the aft end of your boat to be when docked. As a guide to help you drive one of your cat's corners to a target cleat, pick two vertical objects, one in front of the other, such as a dock power console or fuel pump in front of a yacht's mast—to create a transit bearing. As you proceed toward the dock, by keeping these objects in line you'll be following the right course.

BASED ON THE DOCK HEIGHT, set your fenders so that they protect your boat—neither too high nor dragging in the water. Most modern cruising yachts have portlights on the sides of the hulls, so align the fenders to avoid them.

Align fenders to avoid port lights.

COCKPIT CONVERSATION: Have a docking plan and discuss it thoroughly with everyone before beginning the maneuver. Turn off any music or extraneous sounds aboard your boat.

Assign roles—spring line, bow line, stern line, fenders, etc. Agree on hand signals and make sure everyone understands what they should be doing. Encourage them to ask questions if there's any doubt or ambiguity. Only then, spread your crew around to their assigned positions.

Execute your plan using hand signals rather than voice commands because they won't be able to hear you 30-40 feet (10-12 meters) away, over the noise of the engine, other boats, music from the bar (there's always music), and birds squawking.

FACTORS YOU CAN'T CONTROL:

WIND: We live in the air. We feel it around us; we see the effects it has on clouds, water, flags, and trees. We can't control it, but must be aware of it and learn to work with it. Observe wind direction and speed and what the combined effect of these will be on your boat as you approach the dock—and when you've come to a stop alongside.

Check your masthead indicator for wind direction at the boat and the courtesy flags on other boats that are already at the dock. The wind may be entirely different on your boat if you're 50 meters out. And it may be different at deck level than at the masthead. Watch for sudden changes in intensity and direction—gusts, lulls—as you come in. Docks and buildings can create wind eddies and shadows. Some docks are more exposed to the prevailing trade winds. Docking at them with a moderate to fresh wind is like parking a car on a steep hill: if you're approaching downwind (down the hill) you'll need very little—if any—power, as the wind will push you. As always on a catamaran, check that the wind isn't pushing you sideways or off your desired line.

If you're approaching upwind (uphill), you'll need more— possibly constant—low power to keep moving against it.

CURRENT: Current effect is minimal in most Caribbean docking situations. The oceanic current is slight and docks are generally situated in protected harbors. That said, if you do find that you have some current where you're docking, be aware that water is 800 times denser than air, so just one knot of current is equivalent to about 10-15 knots of wind speed from the same direction.

Also, watch out for ferries and other boats at the dock that may be tied up but have their engines running and props turning—they can put out a stream of water more powerful than any current.

> **NOTE**: *When approaching a dock, look for boats similar to yours that are on a mooring or at anchor. The angle at which they lie will reveal the combined effects of wind and current at that position--information helpful to you in your approach.*

OTHER BOATS: They were here before you, so you just have to work around or in between them. If you can't stem the wind directly, be careful of getting blown sideways on to the boats to leeward of your chosen line of approach.

Close to the dock, look for activity on the deck of boats there—people getting lines ready, someone at the helm. A vessel might be about to leave and so make your approach easier—don't be afraid to swing by and ask them.

CHECK YOUR SIX: And always glance behind you. There may be someone following you in.

HELPFUL HANGABOUTS: Yachties are generally a friendly and helpful bunch and will happily put down their beverage to assist another sailor. They do the same for each other, too—it's not that you're an obvious newbie, it's that almost everyone could use a hand. But there is a type of helpful hangabout who is not like these kind folk. You'll encounter him when you come into a dock and the dock-hands are busy or on a break and there are no working mariners around.

He's the well-intentioned, clueless stranger who might be a first-time bareboater, a charter guest, or some tourist just walking along the dock to look at the boats—a doofus on a daytrip.

These people might be fine human beings who just want to help— but can they handle a line, tie a hitch, or know a cleat from a clarinet? If you have a plan and are confident that you can execute it, you can politely wave away their proffered assistance and say something like, 'No thanks. Practicing!'

We've seen well-intentioned dock walkers do the craziest things with dock lines. And bear in mind that you can say the same thing to the dock guys, the professional crew, or the Admiral of the Fleet. They'll understand. But you'd better pull it off!

And bear in mind, most dockhands have seen every imaginable docking variable. They are well prepared, so listen to what they say. If you can't hear the dock master or are not sure of what they're saying, don't just ignore them. Use the phrase 'Say again' if you want them to repeat something.

Give them plenty of time, since there are a myriad of calls on their attention: Guests wanting ice or fuel, departing boats, garbage dropoffs and the like. If you can be patient, the dockhands will be most appreciative. But be ready with your lines in place, fenders attached, your crew dispersed as necessary. That way the dockhands will be able to concentrate on the essentials.

25

Cat Tricks

CONTROL ISSUES

One of the ironies of operating a modern catamaran is that the very things that make the cat arguably more difficult than a monohull to sail—the size of the boat, the distance between hulls, the shallow draft and rudders—can make it much easier to drive under power, and to dock.

Although at first glance it looks like you're driving something approaching the size of a squash court, docking a catamaran is a much easier skill to learn and execute than docking a similar-length monohull.

CATAMARAN ADVANTAGES INCLUDE:

- Widely spaced propellers driven by efficient modern diesel engines coupled with propellers that give a powerful grip in the water. This efficiency means you shouldn't need high RPMs on your engines. *Easy does it* is our mantra.
- Shallow keels and small rudders, so there's not much underwater profile to create resistance.
- An elevated helm station giving a commanding view, at

least on some models. The difference in helm positions makes for big variations on these boats—there is no perfect solution since sightlines are always obscured no matter where the helm is located. Some boats have a high, central, single helm; others have a single helm located to one side or the other. Still others have twin wheels—one on each side of the boat, far astern.

- A pivot point that you control because it changes as you change engine thrust. It moves fore-and-aft/side-to-side as you adjust throttle pressure. It's on the centerline at the mast when equal thrust is applied fore and aft on each propeller.

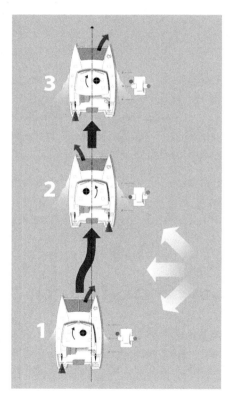

Pivot point moves to side generating least thrust

BUT IT SHIFTS toward the side generating the least thrust as you change throttle position. And you can further change the pivot point with a dock line attached to the vessel at bow, stern or mid-ships.

These advantages can make your arrivals on and departures from the dock less stressful and you will maximize your ability to hover— that is, hold position while you decide what to do next. And should you need to bail out of a maneuver you'll do so confidently and under control.

THERE ARE, however, a few complications inherent in the design of the cruising cat that can impact these close-quarter maneuvers:

SIGHTLINES: As noted above, every model differs in layout. Whilst they all do well when under sail and the sightlines are long, when approaching a dock there will always be blind spots. It's just as well you have crew aboard to feed you information as you get close to the concrete.

SMALL RUDDERS: ineffective under about 1.5 − 2 knots. The same shallow keels and small rudders also offer less resistance to the effects of wind. This relative imbalance of windage to underwater resistance means the boat can more easily get blown to leeward in a breeze.

FREEBOARD: Side decks are much higher than on a similarly sized monohull. Apart from creating more windage, they also make stepping onto the dock from the boat more difficult.

BACKING THE CAT: Driving a cat in reverse is much easier than with a monohull, because the lateral resistance of the two hulls eliminates prop walk. Also, even though one of the two sterns may be out of your sightline, the other will be close to the helm. Work off this side and you'll easily judge distance-off and speed of approach. Station someone to signal distance-off anything hidden behind a blind spot. Agree upon signals with the crew.

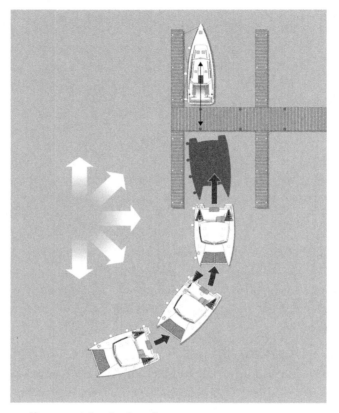

Use a transit bearing for reference

Since you're likely to have only one wheel with engine controls, try to dock that-side-to unless you absolutely can't—at least until you get used to the boat. With practice, you'll be able to dock on either side as easily as you can park your car either side to a curb. But make it easy on yourself initially.

Just be aware that when you are operating the boat from an offside position, far away from the dock, you must position a spotter at the near side to give you precise information as to what is happening in places you can't see.

NOTE: *When driving your boat astern, position yourself so that you're facing in the direction of travel. On most cats, you can stand, crouch or sit forward or to the side of the Morse-style Dual Function/Dual Lever controls —these have the gearshift and throttle functions for each engine combined into a single lever. You'll be able to see where you're going without looking over your shoulder, as you might in your car.*

Driving position with full access to throttles and a good sightline. No need for the wheel.

BECAUSE OF FREEBOARD and sightline advantages, we recommend approaching parallel to the dock, then backing down to get the aft cleat closest to the dockside cleat or bollard. Throw a bight from the boat around the dock cleat or bollard, and bring the line back to the shipboard cleat. This lassoing from the sugar-scoop stern of a cat will be a lot easier as they are lower and closer to the cleat.

To make it even easier, detach the lifelines guarding the aft steps to simplify throwing a bight around the cleat. Just don't let your crew step off the boat. If they miss the first throw, hold the boat in place using your engines only, or re-position until they can do it again. Once attached by the stern cleat, motor ahead gently and the boat will swing easily against the dock.

Go gently on the throttles since your handlers will have both hands full and won't be holding on to anything else to support themselves. An aggressive move on the throttles could send them flying. If, by mischance a line gets dropped in the water at the stern, put the near engine into neutral until it's retrieved.

As MENTIONED, when maneuvering at low speed, you'll find that the rudders are ineffective at less than 1.5- 2 knots. So before you get close to the dock, center the wheel and lock it in place by either a screw-tightened center ring-lock on the wheel or, better, by tying off a short length of line around the wheel. Tie it tight with a round turn and 2 half-hitches, preferably with the last half hitch made on the slip for quicker removal. Some of the newer, larger cats have hydraulic steering and the wheel just needs to be centered, not locked or lashed.

VISUALIZE EXERCISE: Imagine your catamaran as a big airport/supermarket-style trolley. Your hands rest on the horizontal bar. Imagine how you move your hands, elbows and shoulders as you maneuver your trolley around the aisles of a supermarket or around people in the airport. Let's say you want to turn your trolley to the left 90 degrees, but without going forward. You'd push forward with your right hand and pull back with your left.

How much you pull and push depends on how heavy your trolley is and how strong you are. You may be better at pushing than pulling —just like most propellers are more efficient at going forward than in reverse. So, in our example above, you compensate by pulling back harder with your left hand to prevent the trolley from advancing forward. You operate your throttles/shifters when applying differential (opposite) thrust in exactly the same fashion.

Now, with this analogy in mind, there are two ways to rotate your catamaran.

- One speeds you up (forward or backward) as you turn.
- One turns you without speeding you up.
- Which one you use depends on what you want to achieve and how much room you have to maneuver.
- When docking, space is almost always limited, so it's important to be able to rotate the vessel without creating forwards or backwards movement.

NOTE: *Unless it has Max-Prop type folding propellers, when doing a pivot turn on a cat, an engine in reverse will provide about 80% of the thrust you'd experience in forward gear at the same RPM. So, to execute an on-the-spot turn without going forwards, give the reverse engine a tad more revs than the forward one.*

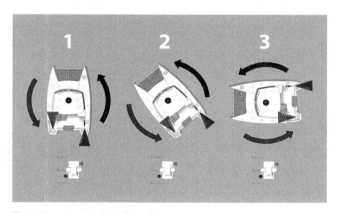

Turn the cat using throttles only.

As you make your way closer to your final approach, keep speed somewhere between 2 and 4 knots. Just enough so you can steer the boat. If your cat is going at the speed and in the direction that you want, let the boat glide with the engines in neutral.

- Use short blips or pulses of power to adjust heading— usually just to the first indent on the shifter.

- Alternate the engines so you 'walk' the boat forward. You can maintain momentum with less speed this way by using gentle blips of power on one engine then the other.
- Don't always use forward thrust to adjust your heading because doing so will make you go faster as you turn— which is seldom what you want when close maneuvering.
- To counter that speed, try using a blip of reverse when re-aligning yourself to your desired track.

HOW IT'S DONE: With your wheel locked or tied on the centerline, here's how to dock any cruising catamaran:

Attach a line to either a bow or a stern cleat and use engines to bring the chosen corner of the vessel to the target cleat or bollard on the dock. Generally one of your stern corners is better—by varying thrust to the near and offside engines you can bring a cat's corner tight into the dock. Be gentle with the throttles, especially if they're electronic—you don't want the boat to surge and apply sudden excess pressure to the dock line.

Using only your Morse type throttle/gear shift controls, make your approach to the dock, preferably using a transit bearing.

Have dock lines led outside of all impediments, coiled and ready for use. Attach fenders, keeping in mind the height of tide and the type of dock. Many docks have boards all the way down to the sea surface, so a fender sitting a few inches off the water is often in a good position. Otherwise, make a dry run first to eyeball the height of the dock and location of dock cleats or bollards. If in doubt, alternate high and low fenders—you can adjust the incorrect ones when you're safely on the dock.

ASSIGN POSITIONS AND ROLES. Aside from the driver, you need one person to indicate distance off, and another with the ability to throw a line over a cleat that will be about 6-10 feet away from the thrower's hands. Practice throwing into the boat beforehand—and use a dry dock-line, as they are much lighter!

- On your final approach, come in at any angle that you can, using your throttles to compensate for wind— even approaching directly into it if there's a stiff breeze.
- Stop your chosen corner about a foot before touching, taking your cues from a crew member in position.
- Get a bow or stern line attached to the dock. Any of your four corners will do, but choose the one with the best sightlines.
- Stern attachments are often best because of the proximity to the driver, lower topsides, detachable lifelines, and use of the sugar scoop as a throwing platform. Make this line as short as you can but it'll still work when a bit long—just shorten it up later when there's no tension on it.

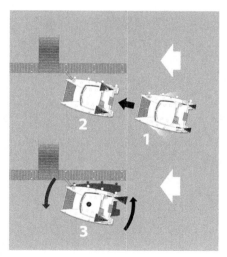

Get a line around a dock fitting and work from that

Once this first line is fixed to the dock, use your outside engine to bring the cat parallel to the structure. Whether you use forward or reverse —or a combination of the two—will depend on which corner you have a line on.

Although we use pulses of power when maneuvering, once you're secured apply steady power to bring your vessel parallel to the dock.

NOTE: *Electronic 'fly by wire' Morse controls require a very gentle touch because they offer little friction-based resistance to the driver plus they have a slight time-lag which can cause the operator to be tricked into thinking they need more power—and then find they have added too much. Remember,* Easy Does It.

26

Cowboy Up
THROWING A BIGHT

When approaching a dock, the best technique for attaching a dockline to a cleat or bollard varies depending on the type of boat. The main difference lies in whether it is safer and easier to stay aboard the vessel than to step off onto the dock.

As cruising boats have increased in size—not overall length necessarily, but interior volume definitely—freeboard has increased as well. This is now as true for monohulls as for catamarans, which have almost always sported high topsides.

WHAT USED to be an easy step down from the deck to the dock is now often a heart-stopping leap, accompanied by the risk of a twisted ankle or knee, the dropping of the line or a staggering waltz around the (inevitable) group of bemused bystanders. So what's the alternative?

The best option is to stay aboard the vessel and throw (or drop) a loop of line—a bight—from the deck down to and around the dockside cleat or bollard, then to secure the free end back on deck, around the originating cleat. The method—the Operatic method—

for throwing the line is often described as throwing a Lasso—though it differs from the cowboy version in that the loop that is thrown is an open loop and not a closed one.

HERE'S HOW:

- First, if your boat has docklines with a pre-spliced or pre-made loop in one end, slide it through-and-over the cleat (from outside the lifelines). If not, make a bowline and do the same.
- Having secured the end to the cleat on board your vessel—at bow or stern on a catamaran and also midships on a monohull—then coil it toward the free end, making several loops of a full arms-length apart and each made with a half-roll (away from you).
- Divide these assembled loops neatly in two so that half of them are in one hand, and half in the other.
- Make sure the line is free to run and not entangled in lifelines or other metalwork.
- There are two ways of casting off your loops. If you're the line thrower, your choice will depend on how close the driver can bring the boat to the target cleat, and your height and arm strength.

THE BACKSWING METHOD:

Let's say that the crew member driving the boat is being very cautious, or hasn't been able to hold you as close to your target as you'd like. Provided you're no further than about ten feet (3 meters) away you can still get your bight home by standing somewhat sideways (inboard or outboard depending if you're right- or left-handed) and employing a backswing to both sets of loops.

Swing Time.

Do two or three swings to establish a rhythm. But make sure that no lifelines are in the way of your swing. On all bareboats, one of the side, and all of the aft, lifelines will have detachable clips, enabling you to have more room to swing your loops. On some catamarans, the forward lifelines are also detachable.

THE OPERATIC METHOD:

This is for shorter throws, where the line-thrower is within six feet of the target. Here, the loops in the other hand should be held loosely as well, with palms facing inward—toward your chest. Now bring both the hands, with the loops of line held securely, together at chest level, just touching the sternum. Then fling both hands out wide, releasing the loops of line when your arms are fully extended. Think of a tenor throwing out his arms at the end of a performance.

The thrower must now rapidly gather the line back aboard the vessel, and having made it as short as possible, quickly make it fast around the cleat it started from in the usual fashion, creating a tight loop around the dockside target—the shorter, the better. But they need to get it on as fast as they can, since the driver can't perform his next maneuver until they do. If on a vessel where the driver can't see clearly, have someone relay by voice or, better, hand signal (a clenched fist) that the line is made.

Practising the Operatic throw.

NOTE: *In both methods, the loops of line are released at the end of the front swing as the arms reach their full extension so that all is released. But the line is* **still firmly grasped at the end by the fingers of the releasing hand**. *Just before you make your final approach, try to practise by making a few dummy throws inboard into your boat to keep the line dry—you'll be surprised how far you can cast! This way, you'll throw with greater confidence of your range.*

AFTER THE REMAINING bow and spring lines are leisurely lassoed in the same way the boat, now secured, can be left with the lines exactly as is for a short time whilst refueling or shopping. For a longer stay they should be retied with the working end on the dock and the other end attached to the boat's cleats.

NOTE: *Never aim* at *your target cleat or bollard. Always aim* beyond it *and you should get it first time.*

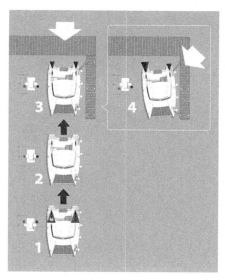

With wind behind, loop stern line around a dock bollard and
pivot off that.

If the thrown line doesn't loop properly around the dockside
bollard/cleat, pull it back onboard and re-throw as described above.
This can be repeated several times—even if it means maneuvering
the boat away from the dock and returning to position it as close as
desired. In this way, there are no crew left waiting on the dock.

27

Beach Buggy

THE DINGHY

The dink, the skiff, the runabout, the Zodiac —the dinghy has many names and many functions. The cheery nicknames endorse just how important the little boat is to the charter. It can serve as a life-saving tugboat as you get blown towards the coral, or a 'funabout' towing the kids on an inflatable tube. But whatever you call it, and however you use it, you need to keep it in good order.

On a catamaran, it should be in davits when you are underway. Secure it well so it doesn't swing back and forth and chafe against the davit supports. Attach lines to the dinghy's bow U-bolt and one of the stern U-bolts and secure these lines to the aft shipboard cleats. If your dinghy doesn't have U-bolts or pad eyes for this purpose, ask your boat briefer how best to secure it. There are many creative ways of achieving this—often using the tail end of the davit lines looped around and back from the leg of the dinghy's engine. Always remove the bung/drain stopper when underway—and secure it to the dinghy with a length of small line.

In heavy conditions, the swell can curl up into the dink and fill it— or at least splash in enough water that the fuel tank will float, and even flip. So tie down the fuel tank in the dinghy—there's often a U-bolt you can use on either side inboard of the dinghy's transom. Heavy rain will create the same problem, so pull that plug.

Brace the dinghy from bow and stern

If you need to bail out a lot of rain water from the dinghy you're towing, hoist the dinghy in the davits and let the water flow out of the drain hole. Be sure to replace the bung before releasing your securing lines and dropping the dink back into the water.

When starting the outboard via a pull cord, you can avoid the common problem of bashing people in the head as you pull the cord by ensuring that you are the only person in the dinghy. When you have it running to your satisfaction, invite the rest of the gang to join you.

And, when refuelling, don't forget which type of fuel it takes—2 or 4 stroke.

EASY FIXES FOR COMMON PROBLEMS:

- Before starting, check that the air vent on top of the fuel tank is in the open position. If not, the engine will start and run but will quit after about 30 seconds.

- The bulb in the fuel line lets you prime the pump—squeeze the bulb until it feels firm.
- Watch that the fuel line doesn't get pinched by the tank lying on top of it. Or by your foot, for that matter.
- If you pull too many times on the outboard's start cord and it fails to start, you've likely flooded it with gas. You can probably smell it too. You'll get it going again if you disconnect the quick-release fuel line from the engine and pull again with the throttle wide open (max revs). It'll likely fire up straight away. Quickly bring down the revs and reconnect the fuel line.
- Whether you're right or left-handed, the dinghy is designed for the operator to sit on the starboard-side tube and steer with the left hand because the tiller arm, gear shift, and throttle twist rotation are all optimized for this operation.
- Have the person sitting farthest in front hold the painter when underway.
- Don't tie-up too tight to the dock—leave room for others to come in. In a busy area, it's a good idea to leave plenty of painter—a full dinghy length off the dock—so other boaters can fit.

Tie dinghy with a long line and leave motor down

- If you have a choice, tie up on the leeward side of the dinghy dock and if there is any chop or swell running, use the dink's anchor, attached to the stern, to keep it from smashing against the dock while you're away or—worse —

getting crushed beneath it. ALWAYS leave the motor in the down position—otherwise you risk having the motor bashed by a moving dink or of damaging someone else's dinghy.

- When operating a charcoal-fired BBQ (most are gas), keep the dinghy well clear (if it's in the water) by tying it off to a midships cleat, well forward of the stern. If the dinghy is in davits, keep a wet towel or a full bucket of seawater close by to smother any stray sparks.

- Beaching the dinghy is frowned upon by almost every charter company—if not specifically forbidden. Surging swell is too great to risk—even if all is calm when you head off to the restaurant, by the time you get back it could be entirely different. Dinghies can get tossed around, have their anchors torn out or be filled with sand and seawater by just a few unfortunate swells from large power yachts.

- Dinghy painters are one of the most common causes of fouled propellers and drive shafts—especially on catamarans with their shallow props, so be extra careful when reversing with a dinghy under tow.

Sand belongs on the beach, not the boat.

- Shake off as much sand as you can before you get in. Once in, trail sandy legs over the side of the dinghy and rinse it all off.

- Once the dinghy's raised in the davits, throw a few buckets of sea water in to flush sand out of the opened plughole. Have a bucket of seawater ready to dip those sandy feet into as soon as you get on the mother ship and before you proceed further.

- Make it a rule that no one steps off the aft deck until they have thoroughly cleaned their feet and legs of grains of sand.
- Even better, have everyone slip out of the dinghy and swim to the ship's ladder, making sure to flush the sand from swimsuits and every nook and cranny while in the water. And make sure the dinghy engine is not running!

Dinghy light. Your charter company should provide you with the legally required white all-round light. Most don't, but supply a flashlight/torch instead—which is good enough. Make sure that you take it with you when you leave if you're planning on coming back to the boat after sunset. It's easy to forget when you leave for Happy Hour in bright sunshine at 1700 and are surprised when it's dark at 1830. As a last resort, turn on your phone (safely within its dry pouch) and let the light shine outwards.

You don't really need the light for illumination—though make sure you don't run over a mooring ball—you need the light so others can see you.

The Kill Cord: Every dinghy comes equipped with a small plastic clip that slips over a spring-equipped pull out knob. To start the outboard, this clip must be attached behind the pulled out knob to prevent it from breaking the circuit and stopping the motor from running. This clip is attached to a plastic lanyard which should be wrapped around the boat operator's wrist (or ankle) whenever the motor is running. If the dinghy runs aground, a passenger slips overboard, the boat hits a rock, is swamped by another vessel's wake or any of a number of dangers should occur, the operator has only to jerk his arm or leg and the clip will pull out of the knob and the motor will instantly stop running.

Not everyone does this, since it seems to be an inconvenience but nasty things can happen in a dinghy—particularly where there has been alcohol consumed—not necessarily by the crew on your boat, of course.

It's the Caribbean. Rum is involved. Be careful out there.

28

Lock 'Er Up

DINGHY SECURITY

Most catamarans come equipped with powered davits that allow the dinghy to be hoist out of the water and secured. Older models may require crew to grind the winches to pull the dink up. Some crew make it a contest tug-o'war-style with competing teams on each davit.

Larger cats might have a platform that gets lowered into the water and the dinghy rested upon it and then raised up level to the deck. Most, though, are raised by lines that attach to U-bolts fitted to the hull of the dinghy—or to bridles that are attached to a set of U-bolts. Why use davits? These are the two primary reasons:

SECURITY: For various reasons—some economic and some just for the pleasure of the thing—your RIB-type dinghy with its 10-15 HP outboard makes a tempting object for thieves. Mostly down-island, but not only there—the (relatively) rich Virgin Islands have their thieves as well as the less prosperous islands to the south.

Charter boat dinghies will sometimes serve as a source of personal transport for latecomers who have missed the ferry. So, if you're chartering in one of these islands, the briefers at the base will alert you to the risks and guide you on safeguarding your vessel. Recent economic and political misfortunes in Puerto Rico and the US Virgins in the aftermath of Hurricanes Irma and Maria might bode ill for sailors there, too.

There are two main security scenarios—when the dinghy is attached to the mothership whilst all aboard are sleeping, or when the dinghy is at the dock whilst the crew is cavorting—sorry, we mean dining sedately ashore.

On the dock, where there are many watching eyes, a basic lock and cable will do—you are really only trying to make your dinghy less attractive a prize than the unlocked one parked right next to it.

When all is quiet in the mooring field and everyone is asleep, the charter-company supplied wire and padlock often will be insufficient deterrence—the wire alone will not put off experienced thieves. Most will carry a cutter that'll nip through wire before you can say, 'Where's the dinghy?' In these places, the charter company will require you to lift your dink up at night before you turn in. If it does disappear and it wasn't secured as we describe, your insurance coverage will probably be useless. Lock it up!

SEA CONDITIONS:

In parts of the Caribbean, passages cross open, exposed waters. In general, the expectation—and prudent seamanship—require that the dinghy be hoist on davits. And it would be hard to think of a reason not to do so.

Some charters, however, hire an extra, large center-console dinghy to add to their inventory. Too large to fit the davits—which are probably occupied by the regular issued dinghy—it will need to be towed on an extra-long painter or bridle. In rough seas, the painter would be extended two or three boat lengths behind the mother ship so the large dinghy could be placed at the base of the following wave but safe from surfing down the face.

Whatever the method of securing the dinghy or towing it behind, regular attention must be paid to the state of the towing line—is it still tied securely or is the knot slipping?

In really heavy following seas there is a danger of breaking waves filling the dinghy and straining the davit lines (called falls). Make sure the drain bung is removed and that there are no items that could block the drain—a T-shirt or a plastic bag can wreak havoc if not removed.

And when at anchor or on a mooring there might be a temptation to leave the dinghy in the water—in case you need it first thing in the morning, or it's in the way of the BBQ grill. If that is the case, secure it to the mother ship by strong cables and locks. A big dinghy may be worth $25,000 or more and they are much in demand—or their engines are—in many parts of the Caribbean.

So, lock 'er up.

Plug'n'Play

POWER POINTS

The electrical conveniences made possible by the generator on modern boats have brought massive and welcome improvements to the quality of life aboard ship. Aircon! Microwave! Big-Screen Video! Watermaker! All amazing.

And the increases in power requirements for the old familiar chart plotters, ice makers, and other devices have made the genny the go-to source for battery charging, too. But often these sophisticated displays and devices are treated with a casual disregard rather than the molly-coddling they deserve—and, frankly, require.

Marine electronics are just as sensitive as those you have at home. You wouldn't dream of simply pulling the plug on your appliances lest you destroy the careful programming you've entered. Same with that color chart plotter for instance: it's a computer, with sensitivities to match. Ditto with the other navigation instruments, air conditioning units, refrigeration and entertainment equipment. Plus, they live near salt water, and other indignities such as spilled drinks, slimy guacamole, goopy sunscreen, and the like.

When first boarding the charter yacht, or when receiving the Boat Briefing, look in the chart table or under the seat nearby for a copy of the electronics manuals. Spend a few minutes learning the basics of how the chartplotter and VHF operate. If the manual has been removed or can't be found, you can easily look the model up on the internet. You need to know how to properly start them up and how to manage the waypoints and routes that have most likely been installed by previous operators.

Disregard all waypoints and routes since you can't be sure of their accuracy—delete them if you have time. Learn the proper procedure for powering up all instruments. When it comes to powering-down these devices, remember to turn off the individual power buttons at each instrument at the helm station. Don't just kill the breaker at the electrical panel.

Equally important, if you're on a boat with a generator, the air conditioning units should be turned off at the individual cabin controls before disconnecting from shore power. The reason to turn them on and off individually and not via the main breaker is that, if left on, when the generator is fired up and the aircon breaker flipped on there's such a huge current draw when 4-6 aircon units start at the same time that the generator will likely shut itself down in protest. They need to be powered up one-by-one with a 5-10 minute delay between each.

———

AIR CONDITIONING IS the big game-changing amenity on the modern cruising yacht. The distribution of the chilled air differs from one model to the next, but may be divided into three zones—Port and Starboard hulls and the Saloon, for example on the typical four cabin cat, where the temperature of the two cabins in each hull is identical. When there are more cabins or an atypical layout, there may be zones for each cabin—meaning that the occupants of each cabin choose their own temperature.

The reality of onboard air conditioning, however, is that it is not easy to maintain a temperature—it's often bone-achingly cold (as the chilled air sinks to the lower parts of the hulls) or barely cool (in the saloon). Make sure you get plenty of blankets at the start of the journey to compensate for the chill.

> **NOTE**: *In your cabins, keep the sun-shields closed under your hatches and the blinds closed to prevent them becoming greenhouses during the day. It'll be a lot easier and quicker for the genset to cool them down at the end of the day.*

Also don't unplug your boat from shore power without first powering down all the heavy energy consumers on board, starting with all the aircon units at the individual saloon and cabin controls and then all the 110/220 volt aircon and battery charger breakers at the nav. station followed by turning off the 110/220 volt AC input breaker or change-over gate. Only then unplug from the power post —after turning that off, too—you don't want any risk of a current arc.

If traveling between islands, check your connectors are the right type.

State of Charge: During your first 24 hours aboard, pay special attention to electrical consumption as displayed at the breaker panel. Not all battery systems on charter yachts are maintained to perfection, so you'll need to make sure your batteries hold sufficient charge to chill the refrigerators overnight if the generator isn't running.

> **NOTE**: *A fully charged 12-volt battery system should be taken to a level of 14.2-14.4 volts initially, if there is no drain on the system. Once the charger is disconnected, the voltage should fall to around 12.8 volts. If the batteries don't reach that level after hours of charging, or if they rapidly lose their charge, you may have problems.*

NOT ONLY WILL you have smelly fish but the low-voltage alarm will probably kick in around 2 am, disturbing your slumber. *A battery system with a level of 12 volts will have lost 75% of its charge and needs to be reconnected to the charger ASAP.*

If you run the generator all night, then batteries should be well charged, provided you have switched on the breaker for the battery charger (We mention it because we have made this error...ah, more than once!)

Associated with all this charging capacity is the necessity, once the generator and engines are off, to conserve the voltage you've created. Turn off any fans or lights when you're not in the cabin. Monitor the CD player and other electronics—are they burbling away in a part of the boat where no one can hear them?

As part of the daily routine, check the status of the batteries from the saloon control panel. If the voltage is below 12v, you'll need to run an engine or the generator to charge up again if you want things to keep working.

And be aware that the recommendation for most charter yachts is that the generator not be running whilst the vessel is underway. The reason being that the water intake for the genny is close to the surface and can easily suck in air—along with seaweed and other substances—and quickly run dry and overheat as the boat rolls in swell. Clearing that mess is a big job and best avoided by not incurring the problem in the first place.

30

Daily Practice
WOPILG: 'WATER OUT, PEOPLE IN, LOOKING GOOD'

Water Out:

Close port lights and hatches and dog (latch) them tight.

Pump the bilges using the 'manual' feature of the electric bilge pump switch. Flick it back to 'auto' afterward.

PEOPLE IN:

Remind everyone it's a boat, not a vacation cottage.

'One hand for me and one for the ship.'

Close all the gates at the side and back of the boat.

LOOK GOOD:

Flags flying smartly

Laundry off the lifelines and safety rails.

Swim ladder up.

All doors, lockers, drawers, fridges, oven doors, secured from slamming about when rolling through a ferry wake or adverse sea conditions underway.

WOBBLE (ENGINE AND GENERATOR CHECKS)

W Water: Check the coolant levels. Check incoming cooling water strainer for debris. Watch for sea grass or even jelly fish in the basket! If you do need to clean it out, first close the seacock (valve) leading to it from the inside of the hull. Don't forget to reopen it afterward! And, if clearing jelly fish, place your hand in a plastic bag or kitchen gloves first to avoid stings.

O Oil levels: Check the dipstick for correct quantity and color.

B Belts: Check tightness and degree of wear.

B Bilge: look beneath the engine for oil or coolant leaks.

L Look around: Check all round the engine compartment for loose hose clamps, filler caps accidentally not replaced by last technician, nuts and bolts etc. Examine all electrical connections for signs of overheating. If anything is amiss, it'll show some evidence. We have found boats with an engine oil filler cap not in place—a disaster if the engine were started up.

E Exhaust: Once you've exited the engine compartment, fire up the engines and look over the side for water gushing out in spurts. If it's not, close down that engine and check that the seacock leading to the strainer is open. If it is open you may have an issue—call the base for assistance. Do the same with the genset, though without main engines running (so you can hear properly).

LOCK, LASH AND SECURE

When preparing for departure, look around above and below decks, checking for weak points in these areas:

HATCHES AND PORTS: The hatches and opening portlights (aka 'windows') should already be closed but now's the time to double-check that they've been closed securely. Pay extra attention to the more common Lewmar hatches, which can be locked on a half-latch that looks secure but which is not watertight (it has a gap to allow some ventilation while keeping vertically falling rain out).

DOORS, DRAWERS, LOCKERS, AND CABINETS: These should already be locked if you're underway. Before a squall hits, make sure that doors and drawers can't fly open, throwing their contents into the boat or at whoever may be down below.

Pay special attention to drawers with knives, and lockers containing glass jars and wine bottles. You do not want to be cleaning up spilled olive oil, soy sauce, and ketchup in a rolling boat.

The common push-button locks on bareboats sometimes don't engage or properly secure their door or drawer. If this is the case, use some surgical tape from the First Aid kit to temporarily do the job.

Tell the charter company afterward so they can both fix the lock and top up the First Aid kit.

Better yet, bring a roll of strong and wide (at least 1.5") masking (not duct) tape to secure drawers, oven door (if it doesn't have its own dedicated lock) and the like. If you do leave some marks when removing tape, try spraying mosquito repellent on the mess and rubbing with a strong cloth.

This stuff will take Sharpie marks off fiberglass tables and other places, too.

Keep everything secure!

HEADS and TOILETS: Drain all toilet bowls of as much water as possible and lower the lid—objects can fall into the bowl easily in bouncy seas. Drain the shower sump, too, since there are often a few cups of gray water sluicing around. Secure toothbrushes, shampoo, and glass items, towels and anything that might fall and get wet or break.

Breaker/Distribution panel: Turn off power to all units that don't need to be on. Lights, fans, and air conditioning units—and any other extraneous electrical equipment. Do leave the bilge pumps powered on in 'auto' mode, though, since the movement will send trapped water sloshing about the bilges to trip the float switches.

31

Sick Daze

STAYIN' ALIVE

Nothing will impact happiness aboard the yacht as much as a bout of seasickness. Not only your happiness--should you be the one suffering--but the happiness of those around you. If you know or suspect that you or anyone aboard is susceptible, then you should take adequate preventative action. Focusing your eyes on close objects is known to set vulnerable people off. So, unless you're sure you can handle it, put down that book (until safely at anchor or on a mooring). And turn off those phones and iPads/tablets likewise).

There are a number of medications available for seasickness but they each have their complications. Many of these remedies will induce drowsiness, lethargy, dry mouth, and other symptoms. The most important part of taking these meds is timing—take them early. Most are for *prevention* of sea-sickness, not its cure. If you feel symptoms, it is often too late to do anything.

The most effective drug seems to be the *Scopolamine* trans-dermal patch. Talk to your doctor first—there may be side effects that won't help your situation. For most people though, this is amazingly effective and has minimal side effects. Every other remedy pales in comparison.

The other common medication is *Stugeron*—which is widely available in Europe, the UK, and elsewhere but not, at this moment, available in the US. You may be able to buy it over the counter in many island pharmacies especially those that either are or were UK or French/Dutch territories..

FOR THOSE WITH occasionally mild reactions, ginger is known to work wonders. Crystallized ginger is good--or ginger in various candy or chewable forms. Straight ginger root is good, too—grate some fresh ginger into soda water or add the ginger to a cup of tea. Some of the fizzy soft drinks like the local ginger beer can be a good stomach settler—but make sure your choice contains actual ginger and not just a synthetic ginger flavoring.

Duty requires we point out that sea-sickness is associated with hangovers and alcohol—it might be best to refrain from excessive indulgence! One side effect of drinking alcohol, of course, is dehydration. Water is your friend.

Should a member of your party come down with the Queazies, get them into the water when you're anchored or moored. A lot of the problem lies in the confusion induced by the rapid movements in all three dimensions as the yacht is rocked by swell and wind. If you are able to stop in a cove and get the crew swimming, the mood generally improves immensely.

If all else fails, ease the ailing mariner into the shade of a palm tree and let them regain their equilibrium—minus the Painkiller.

IN CONCLUSION: The world of bareboat charters is wide and welcoming. There's a place for every taste—from hardcore sailor to laid-back relaxaholic. Some people want to cram in as much action as the day will accommodate while others want to do as little as possible other than cruise from one beach to the next and snooze in the shade. Most are somewhere in the middle.

No MATTER which category you see yourself in, the same rules apply for everyone:

- Be Careful.
- Be Patient.
- Plan your day.
- Know your boat.
- Know the local regulations.
- Be considerate of other cruisers.
- Clean up after yourself.
- Give yourself time.
- Have fun.
- And remember the mantra: *Easy Does It.*

WE WOULD LOVE to hear from you!

Here's how to reach us:

Drop us a line at

info@smartercharterguides.com

ON FACEBOOK:

https://www.facebook.com/CharterGuides/

ON THE WEB:

https://www.smartercharterguides.com/

Credit Dept.

The authors wish to thank the hundreds of students, clients, and colleagues who have been the catalysts for this project. Without their questions, comments, and enthusiastic commitment to the art and science of bareboat cruising, we wouldn't have started the conversations that led us down this path.

We would also like to thank the management and crews of the many charter companies who have encouraged us in putting these books together.

Photography:

COVER: Photographer: IM_Photo/Shutterstock

Interior photography: Michael Domican/David Blacklock /Andrew Lewis

Special thanks to Kim Downing for the excellent illustrations.

Michael (l) and David (r)

ABOUT THE AUTHORS:

Neither of us started out in maritime school. While we have put together a number of instructor credentials and professional qualifications, our on-the-water skills were mostly learned piecemeal—some from friends, from dads, some from Scouts, some from friends, and a good deal from Just Doing It. Much of this taught us the 'proper' way of working a boat and some...not so much.

WE'VE BEEN WORKING PROFESSIONALLY in Caribbean waters for decades, in many capacities—from sailing and power instructor to charter skipper, charter company owner, corporate manager, and professional coach. Between us we've seen it all and done most of it. We've made mistakes, dragged anchor, snagged propellers, bounced off docks and off the seabed—so we know what we are talking about.

If you haven't been aground, you haven't been around, they say. Well, we've been around.

Along with certifications from various boating organizations, we are both holders of **US Merchant Marine Masters'** qualifications as well as holders of **BVI Commercial licenses.**

MICHAEL WORKED on oil rig supply vessels in Scotland and sailed in America's Cup-level competition.

David pottered around on boats as a kid in New Zealand and worked on ocean liners (QE2), ferries (NYC), yacht deliveries (all over).

Although we actually met each other on the dock in Tortola, BVI, we knew each other from afar, having taught sailing and power boat operation on New York Harbor at the same time—waving *Hello* as we sailed by—under the shadow of the Twin Towers. And we survived tugboats, cruise ships, freighters, garbage scows, as well as day-tripping tour boats, Around-the-World racing fleets, and ice on the late-winter water.

That experience led us to want to save others from many of the mistakes and misfortunes that have come our way. And to share the joys and satisfactions, too.

NEED A COACH? Are you planning to purchase a yacht of your own? Sail the oceans blue? Improve your sailing skills? Michael can work with you at your own pace and comfort level to advise and instruct. Find out more at: caribbeansailingcoach.com

32

Links + QR Codes

Here is a link to our website and the pages containing the many other links and references for different Caribbean destinations and varied sources of information:

https://tinyurl.com/4m6263nm

AND IF YOU have any questions or comments related to the material in this book, please get in touch at

info@smartercharterguides.com

NOTE: *(If direct links are not operable). We are using QR codes to point directly to the services mentioned by way of a smartphone or tablet. If you are unfamiliar with their use, check online—iPhones are equipped to read the codes directly from the camera app, while Android and other devices might require a free app from the Play store (we like 'QR Scanner' by Trend Micro).*

QR11

Virgin Islands Guide

Good Moon Farm
BVI

SmarterCharter
Safety Packet

Windguru (BVI)

Deb Mahan
Meal Plan

SmarterCharter
Links Pages

QR12

Carib Security Index

Traveltalk Online

VI Search Rescue

Noonsite

Carib Sailing Coach

Doyle Guides

Printed in Great Britain
by Amazon